Jochen Wittmann

Auftragstaktik

– Just a command technique or the core pillar of mastering the military operational art?

Auftragstaktik
– Just a command technique or the core pillar of mastering the military operational art?

Jochen Wittmann

2012

Carola Hartmann Miles – Verlag Berlin

CIP-Kurztitelaufnahme der Deutschen Bibliothek

Jochen Wittmann: Auftragstaktik – Just a command technique or the core pillar of mastering the military operational art?

ISBN 978-3-937885-58-2

Herstellung und Verlag: Books on Demand GmbH, Norderstedt

© Carola Hartmann Miles – Verlag,
(www.miles-verlag.jimdo.com; email: UHWHartmann@aol.com)

Alle Rechte, insbesondere das Recht der Vervielfältigung und Verbreitung sowie der Übersetzung, vorbehalten. Kein Teil des Werkes darf in irgendeiner Form (durch Fotokopie, Mikrofilm oder ein anderes Verfahren) ohne schriftliche Genehmigung des Verlages reproduziert oder unter Verwendung elektronischer Systeme gespeichert, verarbeitet, vervielfältigt oder verbreitet werden.

Printed in Germany

FOREWORD

From time to time, an extraordinary manuscript comes to my attention which warrants consideration for publication. In his paper, "Auftragstaktik", i.e. „Mission- oriented Command and Control":- "Just a command technique or the core pillar of mastering the military operational art?", Lieutenant Colonel Dr. Jochen Wittmann, a reserve officer of the German Army, increases the cornerstone of the German military leadership philosophy in peace, war and in the international crisis management operations of our time , the "Auftragstaktik", in a broader perspective as a comprehensive leadership and management concept with its seemingly timeless tenets. He presents convincing arguments that "Auftragstaktik", originally developed by the Prussian-German General Staff System and modified for the Federal Armed Forces of today, is also very useful for the international business and administration.

In the German Army Command and Control Regulation HDv 100/100 of 2000, I was responsible for, I characterized "Auftragstaktik" as follows:

"Auftragstaktik is the supreme command and control principle in the Army. It is based on mutual trust and demands of each soldier, in addition to conscientious performance of duty and willingness to achieve the objectives ordered that he is prepared to accept responsibility, to co-operate and to act independently and resourcefully in accordance with the overall mission. The commander informs his subordinates of his intent, sets clear, achievable objectives and provides the assets required. He only specifies details on how the mission should be executed if measures serving the same objective have to be co-ordinated or if political or military requirements so demand. He grants subordinate commanders freedom in the way they execute the mission. This is a prerequisite for taking quick, decisive action and serves to strengthen the sense of personal responsibility. Military leaders are educated to utilise this latitude. The style of leadership and supervision must take this into account. Auftragstaktik presupposes that a superior is willing to accept the occurrence of mistakes in the execution of the mission. Such tolerance, however, has its limits where the accomplishment of the mission and the lives of soldiers are unnecessarily put at risk."

And I formulated the required leadership qualities of a commander who successfully practices Auftragstaktik based on an axiom of the Prussian- German military culture as follows:

"Fortune favours the brave, and success usually goes to the one who is creative, yet straightforward, bold and quick, yet prudent in deciding on a course of action and enforces his decisions with tenacity and appropriate toughness even against resistance. Commanders who wait for orders cannot exploit favourable opportunities.

Indecision and hesitation tend to be more harmful than resorting to the wrong expedient."

Auftragstaktik grants commanders at all levels a maximum of freedom of action. The other services also command and control on this bases. In the armed forces of Germany´s allies, the beginnings of Auftragstaktik are recognizable. Many allied armed forces have tried to introduce Auftragstaktik based on the German experience and adopted it to their specific military cultures. Misinterpretation and misunderstanding, however, very often accompanied this attempt and process, and the intent to use Auftragstaktik very often degenerated to a lip service.

Lieutenant Colonel Wittmann identifies a broad variety of definitions of Auftragstaktik in his literature analysis. Since Auftragstaktik lacks from theoretical foundation, he tries to ground it theoretically in an interesting and convincing manner.

His work has, undoubtedly, extraordinary relevance to the present and future dimensions of leadership in the multinational structured armed forces of today, but also in areas outside of the military sphere.

Christian E.O. Millotat
Major General (Ret) German Army

TABLE OF CONTENTS

Table of Contents	9
Abbreviations	11
List of Figures	13
List of Tables	14
Abstract	15
Chapter	16

1	Introduction	16
	1.1 General introduction	16
	1.2 Field of research	19
2	Basics of the Auftragstaktik and operational art	20
	2.1 Theoretical background and types of conflicts	20
	2.1.1 War theory of Clausewitz and others	20
	2.1.2 Heuristic approach of operational art by Moltke the Elder	21
	2.1.3 The contemporary military environment	23
	2.2 Basics of operational art	30
	2.2.1 Overview	30
	2.2.2 The "German" method	31
	2.2.3 Basic definitions of key terms	33
	2.3 Basics of Auftragstaktik	39
	2.3.1 History	39
	2.3.2 Fundamental concept of Auftragstaktik	40
	2.3.3 Results of literature analysis about Auftragstaktik	43

2.4 Requirement profile of Auftragstaktik as a comprehensive leadership and management concept instead of a pure command technique	52
3 Analyses of approaches using organizational theory	57
3.1 General remarks	57
3.2 Self-regulation	58
3.3 Decentralization and Delegation	60
3.4 Principal-Agent-Theory	60
3.5 System Theory by Luhmann	63
3.6 Concept of Heterarchy	65
3.7 Network Theory	77
3.8 Synopsis of relevant approaches	79
3.9 Auftragstaktik as a comprehensive leadership and management concept for the contemporary military environment	83
4 Conclusion and future research	86
Appendix 1	88
Appendix 2	89
Bibliography	91
Index	100
Acknowledgement	103

ABBREVIATIONS

A	Agent
BAkWVT	*Bundesakademie für Wehrverwaltung und Wehrtechnik*/Federal Academy of Defense Administration and Technology
CF	Canadian Forces
CFC	Canadian Forces College
C2	Command and Control
DND	Department of National Defence
Ed.	Edited, editor, edition
Eds.	Editors
e.g.	*Exempli gratia*/for example
et al.	*Et alii* /and others
EU	European Union
FüAk	*Führungsakademie (der Bundeswehr)*
GO	Governmental Organization
GPS	Global Positioning System
HDv	*Heeresdienstvorschrift* (German Army Regulation)
Jr.	Junior
LOAC	Law of Armed Conflict
MGFA	*Militärgeschichtliches Forschungsamt*/Military History Research Institute
MIT	Massachusetts Institute of Technology
MoD	Ministry of Defense
N	Size of a (statistical) sample/number of items
NATO	North-Atlantic Treaty Organisation
NCO	Non-Commissioned Officer
NCW	Network-Centric Warfare
n.d.	no date
NEC	Network Enabled Capability
NGO	Non-Governmental Organisation
n.p.	no page number

Nr./no.	*Nummer*/number
ON	Ontario
OOTW	Operation Other Than War
P	Principal
RMA	Revolution in Military Affairs
ROE	Rules of Engagement
SOF	Special Operation Forces
UK	United Kingdom
UN	United Nations
US	United States
US DOD	United States Department of Defence
Vol.	Volume
WW II	World War II
ZDv	*Zentrale Dienstvorschrift* (German Armed Forces Regulation)

LIST OF FIGURES

Figure 2.1 - Spectrum of conflict and military operations	25
Figure 2.2 - Comparison of categories of peace operations	28
Figure 2.3 - Military command versus general management versus leadership	35
Figure 2.4 - Cases of application of Auftragstaktik	42
Figure 3.1 - Model of self-regulation versus model of external control	59
Figure 3.2 - Principal-Agent relation and utility maximising	62
Figure 3.3 - Auftragstaktik in context of Luhmann's theory	65
Figure 3.4 - Heterarchical leadership through democratic decision -making process in different systems	72
Figure 3.5 - Heterarchical leadership in a military organisation applying Auftragstaktik	73
Figure 3.6 - Cases of applying Auftragstaktik	82
Figure A1.1 - Overview of complexity science	88
Figure A2.1 - Period of publications about Auftragstaktik	89
Figure A2.2 - Origin of publications about Auftragstaktik	89
Figure A2.3 - Benefits of Auftragstaktik	90
Figure A2.4 - Limits of Auftragstaktik	90

LIST OF TABLES

Table 2.1 – Comparison between OOTW and warfighting — 27
Table 2.2 – Leadership functions and levels of command and conflict — 37
Table 2.3 – Relevance of characteristics of command and control systems — 48
Table 2.4 – Characteristics of Auftragstaktik in context of levels of command and performance — 54
Table 2.5 – Definitions of Auftragstaktik in context of levels of command and performance — 56
Table 3.1 – Applied organizational theoretical approaches — 58
Table 3.2 – Differentiation between hierarchy and heterarchy as forms of coordination — 67
Table 3.3 – Types of strategy with different forms of coordination — 75
Table 3.4 – Synopsis of relevant approaches — 81

ABSTRACT

Is Auftragstaktik just a command technique or in a broader perspective the core pillar of mastering the military operational art, especially in the contemporary military environment? A widespread misinterpretation and misunderstanding lead to a small rate of application of Auftragstaktik in other armies outside Germany. This is also accompanied by a lack of theoretical foundation, which is vital to structure the complexities of contemporary military environment and to decisively improve the understanding and application of Auftragstaktik. A literature analysis considers a broad variety of definitions and concepts of Auftragstaktik. Explanatory approaches of the organizational theory, which deal with the leadership and management of uncertainty and complexity, are applied. Especially, insights from system theory, the concept of heterarchy and network theory give explanations to the concept of Auftragstaktik as core competence in management and leadership. This is supported by advantageous characteristics of Auftragstaktik: delegation, self-regulation, trust, freedom of action, participation, flexibility. Auftragstaktik is considered as a comprehensive leadership and management concept, which strongly influences people as well as institutions. The contemporary military environment, which is often shaped by complex peace operations, is organized as networks with actors of different domains and processes. This environment multiplies the advantages of Auftragstaktik. Therefore, Auftragstaktik is a core pillar of mastering the military operational art, especially in the contemporary military environment.

CHAPTER 1 INTRODUCTION

1.1 General introduction

This paper should show that Auftragstaktik is not just a command technique, but a comprehensive leadership and management concept, which contributes as a core pillar to the mastering of military operational art. A widespread misinterpretation as well as misunderstanding about Auftragstaktik leads to a small rate of application of Auftragstaktik in other armies outside Germany and it is also accompanied by a lack of theoretical foundation. But the theoretical foundation is vital to structure the complexities of contemporary military environment and to decisively improve the understanding and application of Auftragstaktik. Several authors argue that Auftragstaktik grew out of a social and historical milieu, which could not be adapted to US-American circumstances lacking

(1) the right of independent action for officers like a Prussian Field Marshal and

(2) the interplay of highly complex weapons systems and communication technology of current US Army, which creates little room for independent action of operational commanders.[1]

Hughes argues that "as long as Western armies regard Auftragstaktik simply as a policy of short or general orders, rather

---

[1] Robert M. Citino, *The German Way of War* (Lawrence: University Press of Kansas, 2005), 310. Bismarck underlined the superiority of Prussian-German officer's education. But he also pointed out that especially the non-Prussian commanders like Blücher, Gneisenau and Moltke the Elder were the most successful in contrast to the old-Prussian officers of 1806, who lacked the ability for one's own initiative without instruction. Otto von Bismarck, *Gedanken und Erinnerungen*, (Stuttgart/Berlin: J. G. Cotta'sche Buchhandlung Nachfolger, 1928): 42.

than as a fundamental principle governing all matters requiring decisions and judgement, their officers will not even understand what the principle entails, let alone implement it on the battlefield."[2] Millotat argues that in NATO and multinational army corps headquarters the application of Auftragstaktik was often a lip service and Auftragstaktik was replaced by traditional national command and control systems when time pressure or complex tasks appear.[3]

Keithly et al. underlines that operational art refers fundamentally to the basics of effective command and control, like Auftragstaktik, at the operational level.[4] Other authors point out that in business the growing challenges of organizational and technological change caused by complexity require the design of new organizational concepts. They recommend the application of Auftragstaktik, which successfully recognized the effects of a combination of high complexity and high uncertainty and formulated leadership and organizational processes across functional domains.[5] In business, "Command and Control" has a negative connotation implying strict management rules and micromanagement. Military is often considered as hierarchical and conservative in structural manners. The innovative and adaptive side of the military, which is especially represented by the application of Auftragstaktik, is merely unknown.[6] The Swiss staff officers

---

[2] Daniel J. Hughes, "Auftragstaktik," in *International Military and Defense Encyclopedia,* ed. by Trevor N. Dupuy, vol. I, (New York, 1993): 332.
[3] Christian E. O. Millotat, *Das preußisch-deutsche Generalstabssystem,* (Zürich: vdf-Hochschulverlag, 2000), 42.
[4] David M. Keithly, Stephen P. Ferris, "Auftragstaktik, or Directive Control, in Joint and Combined Operations," *Parameters,* no.03, (1999): 126.
[5] Chris Shilling, David Slavin, Eitan Shamir, Igor Linkov, "Enabling Organizational Innovation: Scientific Process and Military Experience," in *C2 for Complex Endeavors* (in press), (Command and Control Research Program, US DOD, 2008): n.p.
[6] Ibid, n.p.

Bühlmann and Braun considered Auftragstaktik as the typical German intellectual "silver bullet".[7]

There is no consistent definition and understanding of Auftragstaktik in the historical and current technical literature. Furthermore, definitions about Auftragstaktik vary between the consideration as a tactically relevant (military) command technique and a leadership or management concept. Some authors argue that operations conducted by Auftragstaktik were a torrent of actions that exploited success not by operational design but only by tactical success.[8] Some others insist that Auftragstaktik is a *conditio sine qua non* to executing military operational art.[9] The differing opinions, interpretations and critics resulted in a broad misunderstanding about the nature of Auftragstaktik. Thus, the influence of the Auftragstaktik on the operational art of developing, implementing and monitoring a campaign with impacts on the military strategy was underestimated. The aim of this study is to prove that Auftragstaktik is

a) a comprehensive management and leadership concept instead of a pure command technique[10] and

b) a core pillar of mastering military operational art, especially concerning the contemporary military environment.

An analysis of characteristics and tenets of Auftragstaktik based on the examination of different aspects of organizational theory should support the understanding of Auftragstaktik as a comprehensive leadership and management concept and under-

---

[7] Christian Bühlmann, Peter Braun, "Auftragstaktik in Vergangenheit, Gegenwart und Zukunft", *Military Power Revue der Schweizer Armee*, no.1, (2010): 54.

[8] Allan English, "The Operational Art," in *The Operational Art: Canadian Perspectives – Context and Concepts,* ed. by Allan English, et al., 1-74, (Kingston, ON: Canadian Defence Academy Press, 2005), 4, 11.

[9] Ibid, 13-14.

[10] "Command technique" is in this context defined as an instrument of issuing orders. Hughes, Auftragstaktik ...,: 328.

lines its relevance for the contemporary military environment. This broader perspective of Auftragstaktik makes Auftragstaktik a core pillar of mastering military operational art.

1.2 Field of research

The study focuses on an analysis of the basics of Auftragstaktik and the question, how it could shape and influence military operational art, especially in context of the contemporary military environment.

A literature analysis gives an overview about the state-of-the-art of Auftragstaktik and its development in recent years; most of them are based on pragmatic and descriptive comments. In this context, it is necessary to analyse current conflict situations, especially in complex and uncertain (coercive) environments. The military strategist Carl von Clausewitz identified uncertainty, ambiguity and complexity as permanent ingredients of armed conflicts. Theoretical analyses can lead a way of organizing the complexities of the real world for studying armed conflicts because according to Clausewitz "principles, rules, even systems" of strategy must fail in a domain where chance, uncertainty, and ambiguity rule.[11]

In a first step, recent research work of organizational theory is used to pave the way for an understanding of Auftragstaktik as a comprehensive leadership and management concept from a theoretical perspective. In a second step, the insights are used to frame the usefulness of Auftragstaktik in context of the contemporary military environment.

Explanatory approaches of the organizational theory, which deal with the management of uncertainty and complexity,

---

[11] Williamson Murray, *The Making of Strategy: Rulers, States and War,* (Cambridge: Cambridge University Press, 1994), 1,7.

and other scientific subjects, are applied. They underline that Auftragstaktik is a core competence of the military operational art and is adaptable to the contemporary military environment.

2 BASICS OF THE AUFTRAGSTAKTIK AND OPERATIONAL ART

2.1 Theoretical background and types of conflicts

2.1.1 War theory of Clausewitz and others

According to Clausewitz, war is executing policy with other means. This fosters the priority of the government over the military.[12] Furthermore, Clausewitz distinguished between the strategic and tactical level of war, which influence each other. Clausewitz claims that principles, rules, even systems of strategy are often misleading in a world where chance, uncertainty, and ambiguity dominate. Everything in war is simple, but the simplest thing is difficult.[13] Clausewitz characterized war as chaotic and uncertain ("fog of war"), containing so-called frictions. The military commander must always take into account that "frictions" severely influence his decision-making process. Frictions are mostly unforeseen and unpredictable events massively influencing military operations.[14] He differed between regular wars and small wars. Small wars are referred to the experiences during the Napo-

---

[12] Carl von Clausewitz, *Vom Kriege*, 18th edition, (Reinbek: Rowohlt Taschenbuch Verlag, 2010): 216.
[13] Ibid., 49.
[14] Clausewitz, *Vom Kriege*, 49. Taleb calls this phenomenon "Black Swan". Nassim Nicholas Taleb, *The Black Swan: The Impact of the Highly Improbable*, (New York: Random House, 2007), xviii.

leonic War in Spain and the phenomenon of guerrilla warfare, which is also covered by his theory.[15]

In contrast, the Swiss military theorist Jomini had a strong focus on fixed rules based on mathematics. His main consideration was that rules and principles could explain the war and are a prerequisite of war planning and warfare. Jomini is related to the attrition warfare, which was mainly conducted by US and Russian Army.[16]

Austrian military theorist Archduke Charles, who was Commander in Chief of the Austrian Army and the winner of the Battle of Aspern against Napoleon in 1809, is considered as an instructor of his Austrian officer corps. He placed strategy always over tactics. He underestimated tactical successes for strategic thinking in an uncertain environment in contrast to Clausewitz. He was sceptical about tactical successes lacking an overarching strategy. His work came closer to Clausewitz' war theory, but is written as a manual - much more pragmatic and less theoretical.[17]

2.1.2 Heuristic approach of operational art by Moltke the Elder

Operational art as military doctrine, while today widely accepted, did not appear until the mid-nineteenth century. Its origins came from the Prussian-German Army, whose Field Marshal, Helmuth

---

[15] Stuart Kinross, "Clausewitz and low-intensity conflict," *The Journal of Strategic Studies*, no. 1 (2004), 54-55.
[16] English, The Operational Art ..., 15.
[17] Rainer Hauser, Erzherzog Karl – Ausgewählte militärische Schriften, (Norderstedt: Books on Demand, 2004): 15. Dirk Freudenberg, "Der Strategiebegriff bei Clausewitz, Jomini und Erzherzog Karl," in *Jahrbuch 2008 der Clausewitz-Gesellschaft*, ed. by Clausewitz-Gesellschaft, 205-215, vol. 4, (Hamburg: Selbstverlag, 2009), 210.

von Moltke, employed the military doctrine with devastating advantage against comparable equipped and organized enemies.[18]

In the tradition of Clausewitz, Moltke the Elder argued that strategy is a system of operational actions and reactions (*Aushilfen*). He refused to define concrete guidelines for military leadership. Strategy was the application of the common sense concerning warfare. He argued that every situation in war would be unique and therefore there was no common rule for war available and verifiable.[19] Moltke favoured heuristics and preferred the use of a decentralized command system (Auftragstaktik), which allowed exploiting opportunities on the operational and tactical level with decisive impacts on strategic decision process. He argued that "no general plan survives the contact with the enemy for more than twenty-four hours."[20] His conviction was that a plan would just endure until the operations have begun, then the plan had to be adapted by ad-hoc decisions and up-dates based on real-time events following the core intent of the (strategic) commander. The (bottom-up) feedback process by the tactical and operational commanders included that the strategic plan if necessary could be revised and re-orientated.

> The commander, who in our days no longer
> leads a closed phalanx but different armies in

---

[18] Albert Palazzo, *From Moltke To Bin Laden - The Relevance of Doctrine in the Contemporary Military Environment*, (Canberra: Land Warfare Studies Centre, 2008) [study paper on-line]; available from
 http://www.defence.gov.au/army/lwsc/SP315.asp, Internet; accessed 04 July 2010, n.p.

[19] Roland G. Foerster, "Das operative Denken Moltkes des Älteren und die Folgen," in *Operatives Denken bei Clausewitz, Moltke, Schlieffen und Manstein*, ed. by MGFA, 19-42, (Freiburg: Selbstverlag, 1989): 21.

[20] Helmuth von Moltke, in Roger A. Beaumont, *The Nazis' March To Chaos*, (Westport: Praeger Publishers, 2000), 77.

different theatres, cannot manage without the independent action of his subordinate commanders. A victory won without – or even against – higher orders can still be part of the totality, for each victory carries with it far-reaching effects. The commander will add it into his calculations, as he does all those other facts that went into modifying the plan he originally conceived and held to steadily.[21]

Moltke postulated flexibility in the hierarchical military system and voted for reasonable exception of the traditional top-down execution system of orders. In this context, Auftragstaktik is considered as a core pillar of mastering military operational art.

2.1.3 The contemporary military environment

Especially after the Cold War the spectrum of conflicts was enlarged by combat and non-combat conflicts below the official level of war, where military activities were necessary. The challenge of asymmetric war and terrorism has overtaken conventional conflict as the primary threat.[22] Therefore, separating military operations into war fighting and OOTW makes much sense, which is also based on legal and political reasons (see Figure 2.1). War is framed by the LOAC and its rules are internationally standardized and accepted focusing on interstate conflicts, e.g. Geneva conventions. The strategic military response in this case is warfighting. After the Cold War the spectrum of conflicts

---

[21] Helmuth von Moltke, in Major Bigge, *Ueber Selbstthätigkeit der Unterführer im Kriege, Beihefte zum Militär-Wochenblatt,* (Berlin: E.S. Mittler, 1894): 17-18, quoted in Robert M. Citino, *The German Way of War* (Lawrence: University Press of Kansas, 2005), 308.
[22] Palazzo, From Moltke To Bin Laden …, n.p.

shifted from interstate conflicts to intrastate conflicts with quite different actors and objectives. Matuszek underlines that norm-conforming behavior by the actors is often not guaranteed in the intrastate conflicts and employed the term "amorphous war".[23] The strategic military response is OOTW. There is no internationally accepted doctrine about OOTW (as well as war), which relates to different use of ROE, scope and definition of OOTW internationally (see Figure 2.1).

The operational military means are combat operations during war fighting and non-combat as well as combat operations during OOTW covering the conditions of peace and conflict.[24] This includes peace support and related operations as well as counter-insurgency and counter-terrorism operations.[25]

Tactical and operational commanders are challenged by differences in OOTW doctrine and national caveats of command. OOTW activities can cover peaceful and violent non-combat operations as well as combat operations. The complexity of the OOTW is mirrored by the many actors and doctrines involved in the "nation building" process, which often leads to a different assessment of the situation on the different levels of command.

---

[23] Krzysztof C. Matuszek, *Der Krieg als autopoetisches System*, (Wiesbaden: VS-Verlag für Sozialwissenschaften, 2007): 43-44.
[24] Canada, Department of National Defence, B-GJ-005-300/FP-000 *Canadian Forces Operations* (Ottawa: DND Canada, 2004), 1-4.
[25] Related operations also include peace enforcement operations, non-combatant evacuation operations and humanitarian operations. Canada, *Canadian Forces Operations* ..., 10-3.

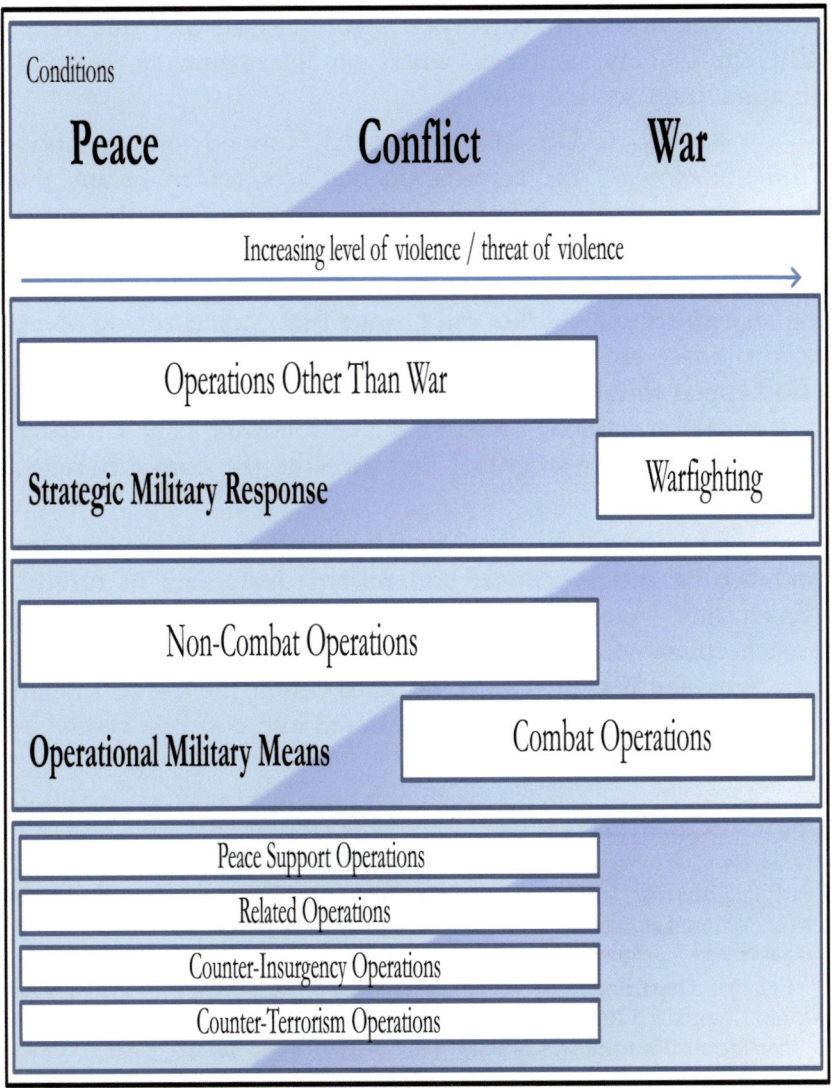

Figure 2.1 - Spectrum of conflict and military operations
Source: Own figure following Department of National Defence, B-GJ-005-300/FP-000: 1-4.

The doctrinal framework is complicated only due to the different OOTW activities, where an internationally, generally accepted framework is missing.

Krulak, a US Marine general, formed the metaphor "three-block-war" for asymmetric conflicts, which means that during an operation different military activities from the use of mid-level military force (block 1: combat) to peacekeeping (block 2) and humanitarian aid (block 3) could become necessary.[26] During an escalation a conflict can change from peacekeeping operation to peace enforcement operation followed by war. This can also happen simultaneously and therefore military forces have to be prepared to operate effectively. The following table compares the OOTW with warfighting and presents the core differences (see Table 2.1).

The Canadian Government underlines the growing importance of peace support and related operations in future.[27] "Small wars"— including counterinsurgency, nation-building, and peacekeeping—seem also to be the major challenge for the U.S. as it fights the War on Terror.[28] Collins counts the last six military operations of US, where the US entered into conflicts caused by humanitarian crises.[29]

---

[26] Charles C. Krulak, "The Strategic Corporal: Leadership in the Three Block War", *Marines Magazine*, (January 1999); available from http://www.au.af.mil/au/awc/awcgate/usmc/strategic_corporal.htm; Internet; accessed 3 August 2010, n.p.

[27] Canada, Department of National Defence, B-GJ-005-307/FP-030 *Peace Support Operations* (Ottawa: DND Canada, 2002), 1-1.

[28] Max Boot, "Beyond the 3-block war", *Armed Forces Journal*, (March 2006); available from http://www.cfr.org/publication/10204/beyond_the_3block_war.html#; Internet; 3 August 2010, n.p.

[29] Joseph J. Collins, "Afghanistan: Winning a Three Block War," *Journal of Conflict Studies*, No. 2, (Winter 2004), 2.

Table 2.1 – Comparison between OOTW and warfighting

criteria	OOTW	Warfighting
rules	ROE, National Criminal Law, International Law	ROE, LOAC, International Law
international accepted framework	no	yes
conflict characteristics	intrastate conflict	interstate conflict
level of uncertainty/ complexity	high	high
level of violence	different levels of violence/ threat of violence	highest level of violence
type of operation	non-combat/combat operation	combat operation
stakeholders	opponent parties, coalition partners, local population, civil authorities, NGOs	warfighting parties, local population
greatest challenge	insurgency and terrorism	war
types of armed forces	specific trained conventional forces, SOF and police forces	conventional forces, SOF

This figure (see Figure 2.2) shows that multidimensional peace support operations, like on the Balkans by EU and in Afghanistan by NATO, are more complex than traditional peace keeping operations, like in Golan Heights by UN, and peace enforcement operations, which are often combat operations.

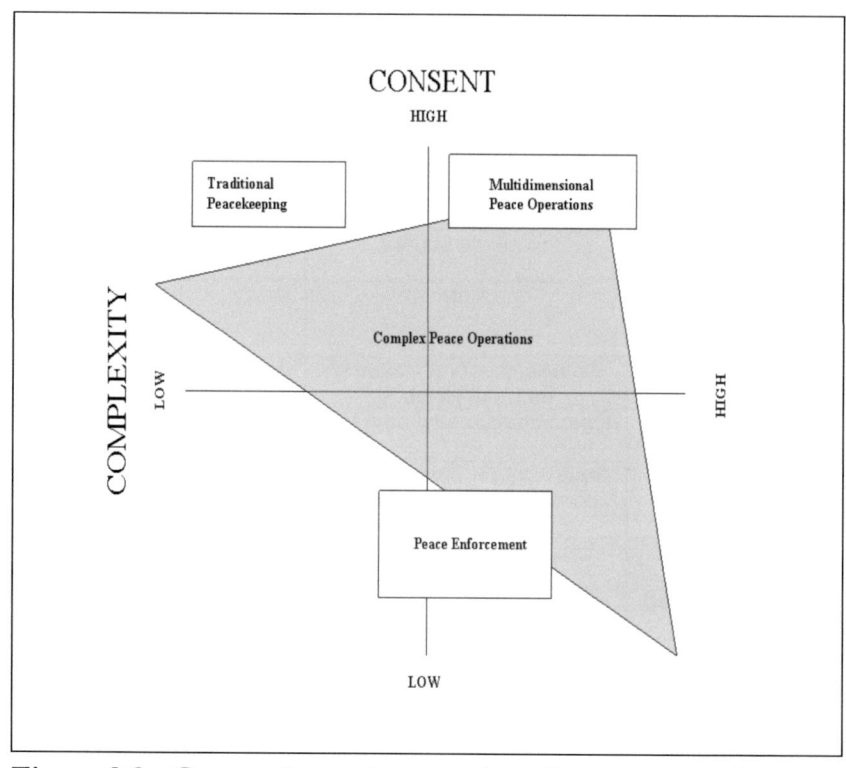

Figure 2.2 - Comparison of categories of peace operations
Source: William Durch, *UN Peacekeeping, American Politics* ...: 8.

Another important development is the mixing of the levels of conflict during OOTW, which has impacts on the operational art. Peskett proposes in this case positive two-way communication, close coordination and clear levels of responsibility.[30]

---

[30] Gordon R. Peskett, "Levels of War: a new Canadian Model to begin the 21th Century," in *The Operational Art: Canadian Perspectives – Context and Concepts*, ed. by Allan English et al., 97-129, (Kingston, ON: Canadian Defence Academy Press, 2005), 122.

OOTW is characterized by many stakeholders (combatants/ noncombatants) and different levels of violence (insurgency/terrorism), which lead to high levels of uncertainty and complexity.

In this context, how could a command and control system like Auftragstaktik work within this contemporary military environment? How does ROE influence the conduct of Auftragstaktik or what is the impact of multinational cooperation during peace keeping or peace enforcement operations on Auftragstaktik? How could Auftragstaktik be helpful for commanders and their subordinates?

The German Army Regulation 100/100 of 1998 rules the following about Auftragstaktik in context of peace operations: "The principles of 'Auftragstaktik' also apply to peace operations but are subject to unique constraints, which often severely limit freedom of action on the ground."[31] Widder identifies several constraints mostly caused by the specific political domain accompanying peace operations. He lists the intense media coverage and especially the ROE of peace operations. He points out that the soldiers receive the position of strategic players, because of the strong focus of tactical activities and decision-making. Further constraints are the impacts of information technology, the micromanagement and the transparency due to the NCW capability.[32] These facts imply that the military and especially the acting commanders and soldiers face new challenges in the contemporary military environment. Multinational cooperation based on different command systems could also be a drawback for leader-

---

[31] Germany, Heeresdienstvorschrift 100/100, "Truppenführung", (Bonn, 15 Oktober 1998): 302.
[32] Werner Widder, "Auftragstaktik and Innere Führung: Trademarks of German Leadership", *Military Review*, September-October, (2002): 6-9.

ship in the contemporary military environment and the involved military personnel.[33]

Some other authors point out the rising relevance of decentralized command and military activity. This gives the tactical level strategic importance and leads to considerations about the "strategic corporal"[34] and "strategic private"[35] in the contemporary military environment. This seems to have an increasing influence on military thinking as well as hierarchical processes and understandings.

2.2   Basics of operational art

2.2.1 Overview

According to the Canadian Forces doctrine, operational art focuses on planning, conducting and sustaining campaigns and major operations to meet strategic objectives within theatres. The tactical forces are supported logistically as well as administratively and provided resources and means by which tactical successes achieve strategic objectives.[36] Military operational art is placed

---

[33] Millotat, *Generalstabssystem* ..., 44-45. Keller underlines that different command and control systems, like Auftragstaktik and Befehlstaktik, should not be mixed in multinational operations, because they are different, non-compatible forms of (military) coordination. Jörg Keller, "Mythos Auftragstaktik," in *Armee in der Demokratie: zum Verhältnis von zivilen und militärischen Prinzipien*, ed. by Ulrich vom Hagen, (Wiesbaden: Schriftenreihe des Sozialwissenschaftlichen Instituts der Bundeswehr, 2006), 150-151.

[34] Krulak, The Strategic Corporal ...,n.p. Jim Storr, "A Command Philosophy for the Information Age: The Continuing Relevance of Mission Command," *Defense Studies* 3, no.3 (Autumn 2003):123.

[35] David Schmidtchen, *The Rise of the Strategic Private: Technology, Control and Change in a Network-Enabled Military*, (Duntroon/Australia: Longmedia, 2006): 9.

[36] English, The Operational Art ..., 7.

between (military) strategic level (strategic goals) and tactical level (campaigns and actions) and ideally serves as a transmission belt between them. "Operational art entails a feel for the troops, a human touch, a psychological connection between leader and led." [37] Therefore, the human factor, like trust, is a decisive success factor to master military operational art.

In general, there are different approaches of operational art in discussion:

The core forms of operational art are on the one side the "orthodox German" versus the "Russian" method according to English.[38] The underlying command and control system, which chiefly characterizes the two methods, are the Auftragstaktik for the German method and the so-called Befehls- or Normaltaktik for the Russian method.

2.2.2 The "German" method

The historical roots of operational art were laid in the 19th century after the Napoleonic Wars in Germany. It could be traced back to Prussian-German Field Marshal Moltke the Elder. According to English, the most conventional interpretation of operational art is executed in Germany. The use of a flexible and decentralized command system by Moltke the Elder severely shapes the operational art, which was (strategically) coordinated by the General Staff. In contrast, the "Russian" method focuses on a centralized command system, which restricts subordinates' initiative and leeway by issuing detailed orders. These orders must be rigidly adhered by unconditional obedience.[39] Critics like Geyer and Naveh pointed out, that operational art in the German context evolved

---

[37] Montgomery C. Meigs, "Operational Art in the New Century," *Parameters*, no. 1 (Spring 2001): 1.
[38] English, The Operational Art ..., 10-12.
[39] Ibid., 13. See also Table 2.3.

as an ad hoc and opportunistic use of force without limits and standard methods.[40] The result of this operational focus led reportedly to the devolving of strategic thought toward the tactical and operational level.[41]

Samuels analyzed the command and control systems of the British and German Empire between 1888 and 1918 based on a comparative approach. He concluded that several aspects made German command and control more effective. These aspects include:

a) the wholly effectiveness in analyzing new developments on the battlefield and in determining its focus (learning aspect),

b) the philosophy of combat, where the infinite diversity of combat made chaos and uncertainty inevitable and unavoidable,

c) a command system which favours consequently decentralization of command using/exploiting individual creativity of subordinates, the ability of low-level initiative and combat skills based on a high standard of training and tactics, which fosters the effective exploitation of tactical and operational situations.[42]

In summary, the one group favours the positive effects of decentralized command system and the exploitation of opportunities by subordinates, the other group criticizes the ad hoc and opportunistic activities and the missing plans and rules.

---

[40] Ibid., 11.
[41] Ibid., 11.
[42] Martin Samuels, *Command or Control?* (London, Frank Cass, 1995), 282-284.

2.2.3 Basic definitions of key terms

In general, Auftragstaktik and *Führen mit Auftrag* are applied synonymously. This work uses the traditional term of "Auftragstaktik". The main reasons are that the term "Auftragstaktik" is widespread and widely accepted and in use as Germanism in the English speaking literature, too. Auftragstaktik covers the characteristics improvisation, flexibility and bottom-up orientation much better than any other definition. Tactic has its origin from the Greek term *tattein*, which means the purposeful leadership of troops, which is still a core task of Auftragstaktik.[43]

There is an important differentiation in military terminology between *Befehl* und *Auftrag* in context of Auftragstaktik and Befehlstaktik. The difference between *Befehl* as order and *Auftrag* as mission, which is part of an order, has a core impact on conducting a centralized or decentralized command and control system. An order in context of Befehlstaktik includes mostly assigned tasks of the higher commander, which are often described in detail and are executed by subordinates without freedom of action; a mission is derived from the higher commander's intent[44] and the assigned tasks of an order, but is not too detailed and grants the subordinate leeway to execute the mission.[45] The core consideration of this definition is that the commander's higher intent weighs much more than the wording of the order itself.[46] The intent is therefore the essential "master plan."[47] This bears a

---

[43] Dirk W. Oetting, "Das Chaos beherrschen," *Truppenpraxis/Wehrausbildung*, no.5, (2000): 349.
[44] The term "common intent" is used synonymously.
[45] Hughes, Auftragstaktik …,: 329.
[46] Franz Uhle-Wettler, "Auftragstaktik," in: Mars – Jahrbuch für Wehrpolitik und Militärwesen, no. 1, (1995): 430.
[47] J.A.S. Cullens, "The Realm of Uncertainty: Directive Control and the Modern Battlefield." *Australian Defence Force Journal*, no. 90, (September/October 1991): 18.

strong behavioral aspect for subordinates to act responsibly and autonomously. In the following it is necessary to explain "command technique" and "comprehensive management and leadership concept" in context to Auftragstaktik.

"Command technique" is defined as a mere instrument of issuing orders. A "comprehensive management and leadership concept" incorporates other core terms, like "command", "leadership" and "management" and contains therefore a broader perspective. The terms are close to definitions according to the manual "Leadership in the Canadian Forces".[48] This guarantees the military context.

a) Command[49]

Command is mirrored in the NATO definition as the authority delegated to an individual of the armed forces for the direction, co-ordination, and control of military forces.[50] Command includes several functions, which covers planning, problem-solving and decision-making, organizing, informing, directing and leading, allocating and managing resources, developing, coordinating, monitoring, controlling. There are additionally the specific authorities of military commanders (see Figure 2.3):

- to apply large-scale lethal force or the threat of this force,
- to command subordinates to go into harm's way, and
- to dispense a specific military justice with substantial powers of punishment.

---

[48] Canadian Defence Academy, *Leadership in the Canadian Forces: Conceptual Foundation*, (Ottawa: Canadian Forces Leadership Institute, 2005): 1.
[49] Ibid., 8.
[50] Ibid., 8.

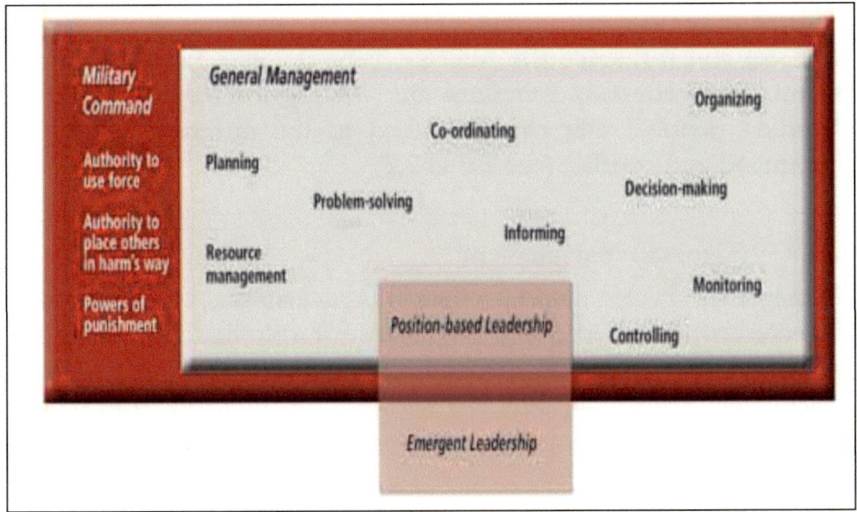

Figure 2.3 - Military command versus general management versus leadership

Source: Canadian Defence Academy, *Leadership in the Canadian Forces*: 11.

b) Leadership[51]

Leadership means to influence others to act in accordance with their intent or a collective purpose.[52] Leader influence may be exercised top-down, horizontally, and bottom-up in a military hierarchy. Leadership can be distinguished between position-based and emergent leadership, which is informally applied within the military organization (see Figure 2.3).

Individuals anywhere in the chain of command are able, given the ability and motivation, to influence peers and superiors.

---

[51] Ibid., 9.
[52] It is called behavioral scientific leadership. Peter Ulrich, Edgar Fluri, *Management*, (Bern/Stuttgart: Paul Haupt, 1984): 139.

This has a bottom-up character and creates flexibility, where ideas can rise and influence the military hierarchy and chain of command. The leadership functions are "leading the institution" and "leading people" that can be linked to the different levels of command and conflict (see Table 2.2).

c)   (General) Management[53]

Management is also based on formal organizational authority, and like command, includes responsibilities for a similarly broad range of functions – planning, problem-solving and decision making, organizing, informing, directing and leading, allocating and managing resources, developing, coordinating, monitoring, controlling (see Figure 2.3).

In the following deviating from the Canadian approach the terms "command" and "management" are used synonymously because of the military context of this analysis. If Auftragstaktik is more a comprehensive management and leadership concept than a command technique, than the aspects of command/ management and leadership must be applied.

---

[53] Canadian Defence Academy, *Leadership in the Canadian Forces ...*, 9.

Table 2.2: Leadership functions and levels of command and conflict

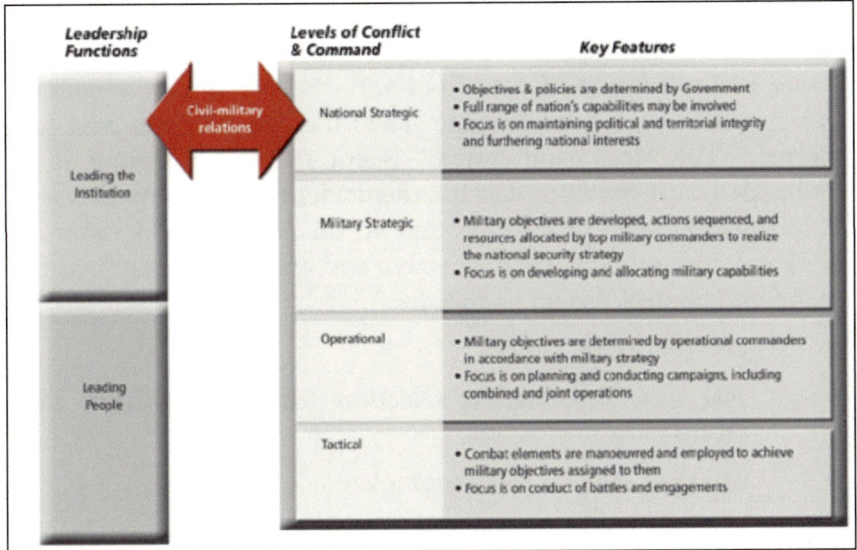

Source: Canadian Defence Academy, *Leadership in the Canadian Forces*: 12.

d) Command and control system[54]

According to van Creveld, a command and control system includes "responsibilities of command", which are divided into two parts:[55]

The first function-related part covers the arrangement and coordination issues which the army needs for existence: food supply, military judicative, medical service and so on.

---

[54] Command and control system is used in this context just as a technical term.
[55] Martin van Creveld, "Introduction: On Command," in *Command in War*, 1-16, (London: Harvard University Press, 1985): 6.

The second output-related part refers to all things necessary to complete the army's mission, e.g. intelligence as well as planning and monitoring operations. This takes into account the minimax principle, which targets on a minimum of own losses and maximum of casualities and destruction of the enemy during the shortest possible time. The functions on command are eternal.[56] The "command system" is not an isolated system, it is embedded into the complex interdependencies of many factors, e. g. organizations, procedures and so on. Van Creveld summarizes the core aspects of an effective and efficient ("ideal") command and control system as follows:[57]

- complexity reduction
- real time information selection (e.g. leading from the front)
- acting as durable force multiplier
- realizing minimax principle (cost-benefit ratio)
- accomplishing missions (e.g. breaking enemy's will)
- adaptability/flexibility

A command and control system according to van Creveld has strong links to management and leadership issues, like information, planning, monitoring, coordinating, and decision-making, resource management and leading.

---

[56] Martin van Creveld, "Conclusions: Reflections on Command," in *Command in War*, 261-275, (London: Harvard University Press, 1985): 265.
[57] Martin van Creveld, Introduction …, 1-16.

2.3 Basics of Auftragstaktik

2.3.1 History

Approaches of the application of Auftragstaktik could be traced back to the beginning of the 19th century, where it was developed by the Prussians after the defeats of Jena and Auerstedt in Thuringia (1806).[58] It was documented in Field Manuals of the Prussian-German Infantry in 1888, the first time. The development of Auftragstaktik lasted several decades and was broadly accepted at the end of the 19th century in the German Army[59] despite prominent opponents like the philosopher Hegel, who postulated the unconditional obedience of the soldier to the state and its aims.[60] Initiative as well as independent leadership and activities by subordinated leaders and soldiers could be identified earlier, especially in the navy, where the captains received a wider leeway because of the great distances[61] or in *Jäger* units of the Hessian and Prussian Army in the 18th century, who did not fight along with the linear tactics of line infantry.[62] As Frederick the Great stated: "your boss issues an instruction, you just have to think about, if you should attack or retreat pending on the circumstances."[63]

---

[58] Stephan Leistenschneider, *Auftragstaktik im preußisch-deutschen Heer 1871-1914*, (Hamburg: Mittler, 2002): 25-35. Millotat also refers to other roots of Auftragstaktik. Millotat, *Generalstabssystem ...*, 42.
[59] Dirk W. Oetting, *Auftragstaktik: Geschichte und Gegenwart einer Führungskonzeption*, (Frankfurt / Bonn: Report-Verlag, 1993): 22-24.
[60] Manfred Messerschmidt, "Denken auf den Krieg hin," *Militärgeschichte*, no. 2 (2010): 5.
[61] Michael Arnold, "Auftragstaktik: Entwicklung und Bedeutung eines Führungsverständnisses", *Allgemeine Schweizerische Militärzeitschrift*, no.12, (2003): 11.
[62] Peter Paret, *Yorck and the era of Prussian reform 1807-1815*, (Princeton: Princeton University Press, 1966): 29-30.
[63] Oetting, *Auftragstaktik...*, 22.

2.3.2 Fundamental concept of Auftragstaktik

The Auftragstaktik is generally focused on the relation between a superior commander and his subordinate. Several core concepts complete the Auftragstaktik:[64]

In the first step, the higher commander's intent (*Absicht*) describes the concept of conducting his plans for a campaign/battle, which is essential. The subordinate commander receives an order including the higher commander's intent and the implied tasks from his superior. The subordinate analyses the higher commander's intent and the implied tasks and identifies his mission (*Auftrag*). Furthermore, he analyzes the broad, local and geographical complexities of the situation (*Lage*). Together, the higher commander's intent, the implied tasks, the mission and the situation produce a need for action (*Problem*). Considering all four criteria, the subordinate reaches a resolution/decision (*Entschluss*) of the need of action.

The tenets relevant to the subordinate commander are the following:[65]

- emphasis on speed in adjusting to new circumstances
- emphasis on speed in maintaining the initiative
- better to make a mistake in a resolution than to delay and reach no resolution
- willingly accept the responsibility for independent decisions
- authorization for abandoning the task when necessary as long as the subordinate commander acted according to the higher commander's intent.

---

[64] Hughes, Auftragstaktik …, 329.
[65] Uhle-Wettler, Auftragstaktik …, 427-428, 434-435.

The deviation from an order is only allowed by the subordinate, when the following criteria are sufficient:[66]

a) The situation has significantly changed or a completely new situation occurred.

b) Immediate action is urgent.

c) The higher commander is not available (in time).

d) The higher commander must be informed if deviating from order as soon as possible without reasoning.[67]

The leeway of the subordinate concerning Auftragstaktik is exemplified in three cases (see Figure 2.4).[68]

a) The first scenario covers the case, that the higher commander's intent, including his assigned tasks are congruent to the analyzed situation by the subordinate (commander). This is the ordinary case.

b) The second scenario includes the case that the higher commander's assigned task of order is not congruent to the analyzed situation by the subordinate (commander). In this case, the subordinate (commander) can deviate from the order under specific circumstances.

c) The third scenario includes the case that a completely new situation occurs, like an airborne landing or an ambush/ a coup de main by insurgents, which requires immediate action by the subordinate (commander).

---

[66] Oetting, Das Chaos beherrschen …, 353.
[67] Gert von Kortzfleisch, "Militärorganisation," in: *Handwörterbuch der Organisation*, ed. by Erwin Grochla, (1969): 997.
[68] Oetting, *Auftragstaktik …*, 235.

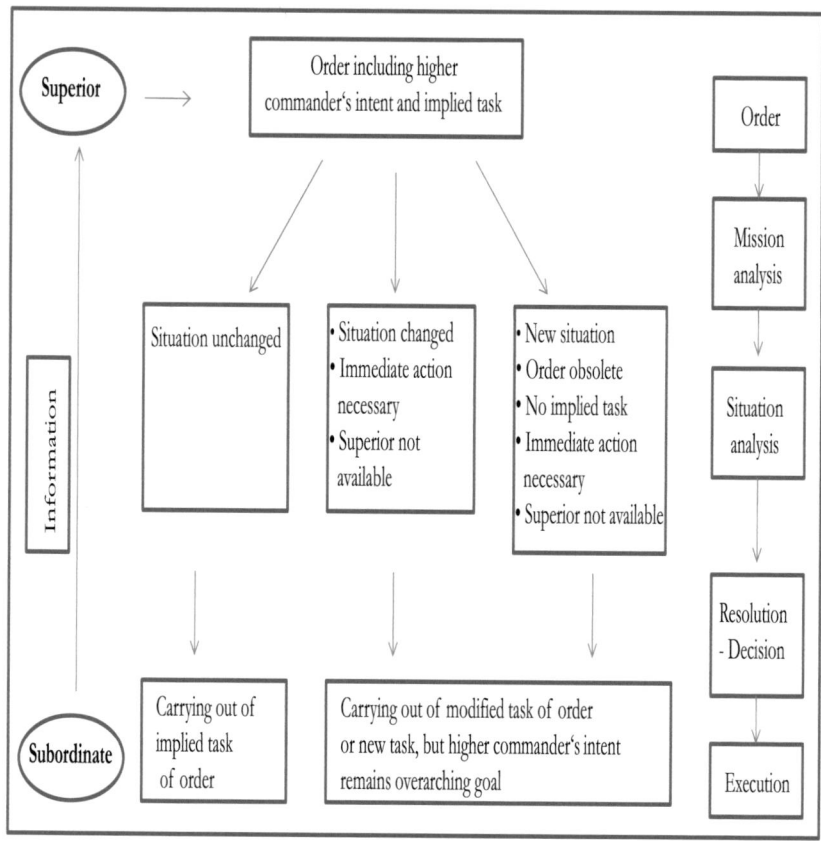

Figure 2.4 - Cases of application of Auftragstaktik

The effectiveness of Auftragstaktik also depends on the harmonization of other important factors: training, officer/NCO selection and promotion, education, grievance system, principal-agent relationship.[69]

---

[69] Hughes, Auftragstaktik ..., 330.

2.3.3 Results of literature analysis about Auftragstaktik

a) Results of the (empirical) study of Auftragstaktik

The basics of the literature study are the search results of more than 132 single sources by the FüAk, Hamburg, the BAkWVT, Mannheim, and the CFC, Toronto (see Appendix 2). The selection criteria were the items "Auftragstaktik", "Führen mit Auftrag", "Mission Command", "Mission-type Tactics" and "Directive Control" in order to search for a wide range of sources.

The collection is representative, because the search at FüAk and BAkWVT includes all relevant libraries within the Bundeswehr, e.g. the library of the MGFA, one of the most reputed military science libraries in the German speaking Europe. Both institutions have strong links to familiar and partner institutions abroad. It is similar with the Canadian Forces College, which has strong links to US-American and Commonwealth resources. The most sources about Auftragstaktik represent German authors (67%), followed by US-American (17%), then Swiss (5%), Canadian (4%), British, Austrian and Australian (2%) and last but not least Dutch, French and Russian authors (1%). Most of the sources are published after 2000 (70%), but also in the nineties (16%), eighties (10%), seventies (2%) as well as fifties and sixties (2%). The historical examples cover the period until the WW II. The current examples focus after the Cold War. The historical and current examples include 22 and 21 sources (of 132 sources). Peace operations, stabilization operations, joint operations as well as domestic operations are more and more relevant for Auftragstaktik.

b) Definitions of Auftragstaktik

There are different classifications of Auftragstaktik. The level of command of the Auftragstaktik is mostly concentrated on the operational and tactical level. Different aspects are involved. Different definitions could be identified:

- Auftragstaktik as a command technique[70]

  The authors favouring Auftragstaktik as a command technique are mostly engaged in the tactical level of command, where the pure application of Auftragstaktik is in the focus of tactical operations.

- Auftragstaktik as a command philosophy[71]

  Authors using Auftragstaktik as a command philosophy often recognize that beside the application on the tactical and operational level, Auftragstaktik is linked with soft factors like self-confidence, reliance and trust. Uhle-Wettler summarizes that Auftragstaktik is the willingness to act independently and the ability to act rationally, but he rejects that Auftragstaktik is based on a philosophy.[72]

- Auftragstaktik as a coordination method/concept in order to reduce complexity[73]

  Keller focuses on a system view with an input-output-mechanism. The idea behind this definition is that the organization applying Auftragstaktik is organized as a system and system theoretical tenets could be used to describe the basics and goals of Auftragstaktik much better.

---

[70] Antulio J. Echevarria, "Auftragstaktik: In Its Proper Perspective," *Military Review*, (October 1986): 50. Hughes, Auftragstaktik ..., 332.

[71] M. B. O'Brien, "Directive Control – The Command Panacea?" *Defence Force Journal*, no. 83, (July/August 1990): 2. John L. Silva, "Auftragstaktik: Its Origin and Development," *Infantry*, (September/October 1989): 6. Storr, A Command Philosophy ..., 119.

[72] Uhle-Wettler, Auftragstaktik ..., 424, 435.

[73] Keller, Mythos Auftragstaktik ..., 160.

- Auftragstaktik as a management method/concept[74]

  Authors often compare this command and control method with management tools/concepts from business and administration. They include leadership issues, training issues and organizational issues into the concept. of Auftragstaktik.

- Auftragstaktik as a delegation method[75]
- Auftragstaktik as learning method[76]

  Auftragstaktik fosters learning effects which are necessary to master the high requirements of initiative, self-reliance … and finally select the best leaders. There is no "school solution" and the leader learns maximum flexibility to perform his duties within the bounds of commander's intent.[77]

- Auftragstaktik as a leadership model[78]

  Manstein traced the German victories back to the highly successful *Führungsgrundsätze* (tenets of leadership): to conduct flexible operations and to give leeway to the leaders of all levels for initiative and independent actions.[79] Widder understands Auftragstaktik as a type of

---

[74] Ivan Yardley, "Crossing the Void, War and Business: Utility of British Military Management Methods beyond the Military," *Defence Studies* 9, no.1 (March 2009): 5. Shilling, Enabling Organizational Innovation …, n.p.

[75] Karl Eckhart, "Auftragstaktik zwischen Delegation und Mandat," *Allgemeine Schweizerische Militärzeitschrift*, no.01/02, (2008): 23.

[76] Gian-Paolo Curcio, "Auftragstaktik im Licht einer pädagogischen Handlungsstruktur," *Allgemeine Schweizerische Militärzeitschrift*, no.12, (2004): 11.

[77] Frank A. Kerkemeyer, "Auftragstaktik," *Infantry*, no.06 Nov./Dec., (1987): 30.

[78] Widder, Auftragstaktik …, 6.

[79] Oetting, *Auftragstaktik* …, 21.

leadership, which is based on a specific role of the soldier as independent acting person. [80]

- Auftragstaktik as a self-regulating or self-monitoring tool[81]

  Ungerer is an expert of stress research and therefore counts on insights of psychology concerning Auftragstaktik and self-regulation.

- Auftragstaktik as a lifestyle[82]

  Hughes points out that a specific esprit de corps of officers and NCO based on the conviction to act independently is a *conditio sine qua non* and enabler of Auftragstaktik.

- Auftragstaktik as a core pillar of mastering the military operational art[83]

The definitions of Auftragstaktik range from the characterization as mere command technique to a leadership or management concept. This mirrors the different understandings about Auftragstaktik. The literature analyses underlines that Auftragstaktik is not a mere command technique, because most of the definitions are linked to Auftragstaktik as a leadership and/or management concept, which incorporates a broader and comprehensive perspective. There are further analyses on the characteristics of Auftragstaktik necessary to support the thesis that Auftragstaktik is a comprehensive management and leadership concept instead of a mere command technique.

---

[80] Widder, Auftragstaktik ..., 6.
[81] Dietrich Ungerer, *Der militärische Einsatz* (Potsdam: miles-Verlag, 2003), 35.
[82] Hughes, Auftragstaktik ..., 332.
[83] English, The Operational Art ..., 11, 13-14.

c) Characteristics of Auftragstaktik

The characteristics of Auftragstaktik are elements of the definitions. The following table represents an overview (ideal case) about the relevance of core characteristics of Auftragstaktik versus Befehlstaktik, because one of the common ways of thinking about Auftragstaktik is to contrast it with Befehlstaktik (see Table 2.3):

Table 2.3 – Relevance of characteristics of command and control systems

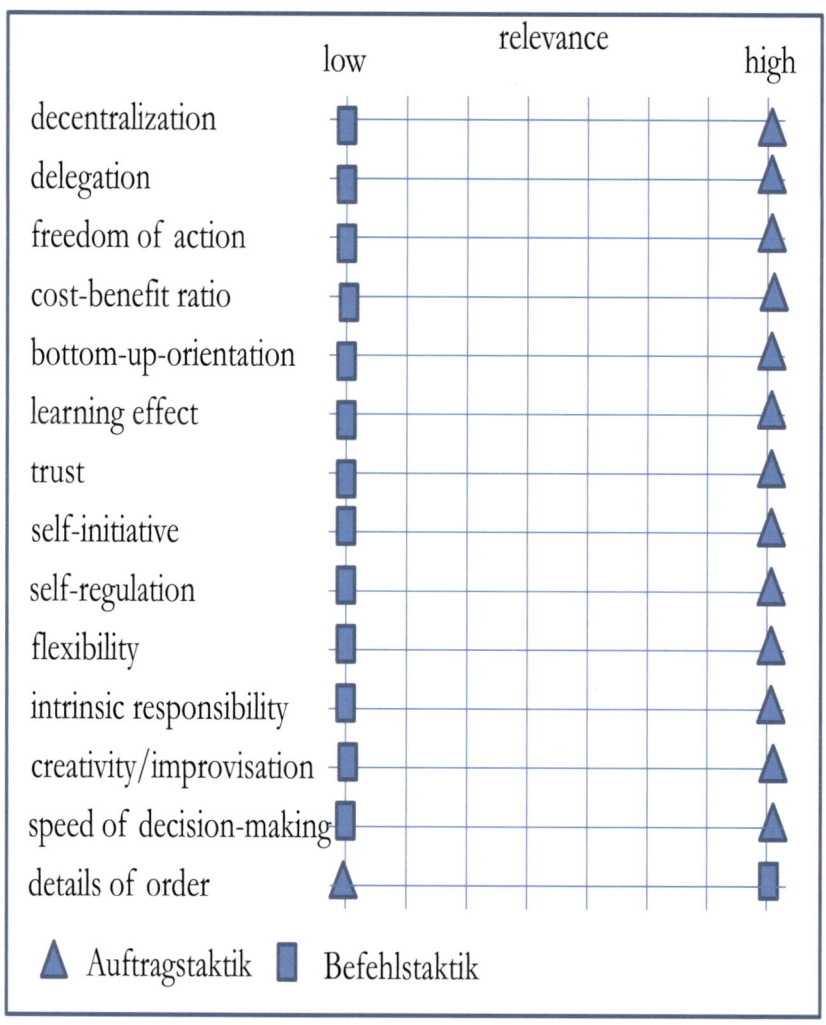

d) Application and implementation of Auftragstaktik and its strategic relevance

Auftragstaktik is partly applied in different countries. During the Cold War, the US introduced consequently aspects of Auftragstaktik with the introduction of manoeuvre warfare.[84] But there are efforts to limit the use of Auftragstaktik because of the new NCW environment and the intention to install a centralized command system.[85] Other authors underline the importance of NCW for the efficient application of Auftragstaktik through real-time information and the improvement of situational awareness of the leaders and troops.[86] Davis and Freudenberg stated that the British Army took over elements of Auftragstaktik into its Field Manual.[87] Storr underlined that the originally tactical interpreted Auftragstaktik is enhanced by a "contract of trust" between superior and subordinate, which makes the understanding and the application easier.[88]

---

[84] English, The Operational Art ..., 34-36.
[85] Robert L. Bateman, "Force XXI and the Death of Auftragstaktik," *Armor*, (January/February 1996): 15.
[86] J. S. Meiter, "Network Enabled Capability: A Theory Desperately in Need of Doctrine, " *Defence Studies*, no. 2 (June 2006): 205. William M. Connor, " Emerging Army Doctrine: Command and Control," *Military Review*, (March/April 2002): 82.
[87] R. R. Davis, "Helmuth von Moltke and the Prussian-German Development of a Decentralized Style of Command: Metz and Sedan 1870", *Defence Studies*, no. 1 (March 2005): 94. Dirk Freudenberg, "Die Rezeption deutschen Führungsdenkens im britischen Führungsverständnis unter besonderer Berücksichtigung von 'Auftragstaktik' und 'Innerer Führung'," in *Jahrbuch 2009 der Clausewitz-Gesellschaft*, ed. by Clausewitz-Gesellschaft, 268-287, vol. 5, (Hamburg: Selbstverlag, 2009), 275-276.
[88] Storr, A Command Philosophy ..., 120.

A Norwegian study shows that Auftragstaktik is an ideal and the autonomy of subordinates is less than the autonomy of superiors in military organization.[89]

A Dutch study about the application of Auftragstaktik during peace operations concludes that imprecise commander's intents and lacking trust between superiors and subordinates led to failures.[90]

In most of the countries applying Auftragstaktik, two main elements and effects, which are necessary for the exploitation of opportunities by subordinates and their motivation, are not considered:

a) the case of deviation from a given order and
b) the impacts of tactical success on operational and strategic level of command.

The Auftragstaktik as core competence and success factor for the operational art is only partly exploited in other countries.

Shilling et al. points out the following prerequisites and conditions for the application of Auftragstaktik:[91]

1. The complexity and chaotic nature of the battlefield, what Clausewitz summarized as 'fog of war', 'friction' and 'uncertainty', are characteristic of conflicts and must be respected.
2. The mission of military commanders is to understand how complex systems function through the idea of common intent and how to optimise subunits mission success

---

[89] Audun Offerdal, Jan O. Jacobsen, "Auftragstaktik in the Norwegian Armed Forces," *Defense Analysis*, vol.9, no. 2 (1993): 221.
[90] Ad L. W. Vogelaar, Eric-Hans Kramer, "Mission Command in Dutch Peace Support Missions," *Armed Forces & Society*, (Spring 2004), 423.
[91] Shilling, Enabling Organizational Innovation ..., n.p.

3. Time is always a critical factor, especially at the operational and tactical level of command, and therefore the decision making processes must be quick.
4. The span of command is limited because even the best commander has a limited capacity of information processing and has to share burden with a limited number of subordinates.
5. The capacity of creativity and improvisation is uniquely human. Technology, regardless of its complexity, can only enhance communication and more efficiently process information.
6. Active participation and an individual sense of executing one's own plan and ideas by subordinates lead to better motivation and commitment. This leads to a mutual learning and experience curve.

e) Advantages and disadvantages of Auftragstaktik

The literature analysis considers several benefits and shortfalls of Auftragstaktik, which are shortly explained. Vogelaar et al. identify four success factors for the application of mission command: autonomy of action, clear objectives, appropriate means and especially mutual trust.[92] Storr underlines the important feature of trust and talks of a "contract of trust" between the superior and subordinate commander.[93] Such latitudes, based on trust and initiative, accelerate production, dissemination and comprehension of orders. Benefits of the Auftragstaktik are therefore the form of delegation, the self-reference of the soldiers, the trust, responsi-

---

[92] Vogelaar, Kramer, Mission Command ..., 423.
[93] Storr, A Command Philosophy ..., 120.

bility and independence, the self-initiative and the cost-benefit-ratio.

The following factors are considered as limits/drawbacks to the application of Auftragstaktik: Bureaucracy, ROE, multinationality in combination with the use of Befehlstaktik, political caveats, superior's micromanagement, information overload by information technology and NCW, the influence of mass media and the criminal law, which has relevance during stabilization operations.[94]

2.4 Requirement profile of Auftragstaktik as a comprehensive leadership and management concept instead of a pure command technique

The relevant considerations of the theoretical foundations and the literature analysis could be summarized as follows:

- The current operating environment is shaped by a high level of uncertainty and complexity.

- The current operating environment makes the strategic importance of tactical decison-making clear and shows more and more a mixing of the levels of conflict, which requires improved concepts of coordination and communication concerning all levels of military organization.

- The current operating environment makes a decentralized command and control system appropriate for countering growing complexity and uncertainty.

---

[94] O'Brien, Directive Control, ... 9. Widder, Auftragstaktik ..., 6-9. Millotat, *Generalstabssystem* ..., 44-45.

- Auftragstaktik is considered in a broader perspective in the technical literature than as a pure command technique.
- Mastering operational art, especially of the current operating environment, requires Auftragstaktik as a comprehensive leadership and management concept, which covers all levels of command as well as all participants in the military leadership process.

The requirement profile of Auftragstaktik can be derived from the characterictics of Auftragstaktik and the requirements to meet the relevant aspects of leadership and management issues.

The characteristics of Auftragstaktik are except the speed of decision-making and the details of order constituent and essential to Auftragstaktik. They just have low or no relevance to Befehlstaktik. The identified characteristics of Auftragstaktik can be traced to relevant levels of command and performance. This is necessary to measure the relevance of them and their reach for leadership and management within the military organization. The following synopsis summarizes the different characteristics of Auftragstaktik (see Table 2.4).

Another aspect is the opportunity to measure performance and effectiveness of individuals, groups and institutions with the characteristics of Auftragstaktik as success factors. Authors like English and Keithly et al. point out the predominant role of an effective decentralized command and control system to the operational art.[95]

---

[95] English, The Operational Art ..., 13-14. Keithly, Auftragstaktik ..., 126.

Table 2.4 - Characteristics of Auftragstaktik in context of levels of command and performance[96]

characteristics of Auftragstaktik	level of command & conflict			level of performance & effectiveness		
	tactical	operational	strategic	individual	group	institution
decentralization	x	x		x	x	
delegation	x	x		x	x	
freedom of action	x	x		x	x	
cost-benefit-ratio	x	x	x	x	x	x
bottom-up-orientation/participation	x	x		x	x	
learning effect	x	x	(x)	x	x	(x)
trust	x	x	x	x	x	x
self-initiative	x	x		x	x	
self-regulation	x			x		
flexibility	x	x	(x)	x	x	(x)
intrinsic responsibility	x			x		
creativity/improvisation	x	x	(x)	x	x	(x)
speed of decision-making	x	x	x	x	x	x
low details of order	x	x	x	x	x	x

[96] Legend: x relevant; (x) partly relevant.

The operational art understood as transmission belt between the strategic and tactical level of command requires a management and leadership concept, which connects all three levels of command as well as performance in order to reduce effectively complexity and uncertainty and act as a force multiplier with inherent flexibility and adaptability, especially in the new operating environment.

The definitions of Auftragstaktik are therefore analyzed concerning the relevance for the levels of command and performance. Six out of ten definitions are selected because they cover core aspects for a comprehensive leadership and management concept (*). The results of the analysis point out that Auftragstaktik has impacts on the strategic as well as the operational and tactical level of command (see Table 2.5).

Further on, the selected definitions should be deeper analyzed in context of organizational theoretical approaches, which refer to management and leadership issues, too. This fosters the theoretical foundation of Auftragstaktik as a comprehensive leadership and management concept. This is also vital to decisively improve the understanding and application of Auftragstaktik, to structure the complexities of contemporary military environment and to install flexibility and adaptability in the leadership and management processes.

Table 2.5 – Definitions of Auftragstaktik in context of levels of command and performance[97]

Auftragstaktik as	level of command & conflict			level of performance & effectiveness		
	tactical	operational	strategic	individual	group	institution
command technique	x	x		x	x	
command philosophy	x	x		x	x	
coordination method/concept *	x	x	x	x	x	x
management method/concept*	x	x	x	x	x	x
delegation method*	x	x	(x)	x	x	(x)
learning method*	x	x	(x)	x	x	(x)
leadership model*	x	x		x	x	
self-regulating tool*	x			x		
lifestyle	x	(x)		x	(x)	
method of (mastering) the military operational art	x	x	x	x	x	x

[97] Legend: x relevant; (x) partly relevant.

3 ANALYSES OF APPROACHES USING ORGANIZATIONAL THEORY

3.1 General remarks

The vast majority of sources about Auftragstaktik are of descriptive nature focussing on military experiences of tactical and operational command levels. Just a few authors refer to theoretical considerations of organizational theory, pedagogy, law and sociology, e.g. English and Oetting recommend the chaos theory for further analyses.[98] The reduction of complexity is, according to van Creveld, the core task of a command system. Therefore a focus on complexity science as part of organizational theory is relevant for further analyses. The legal aspects are later discussed in context with peace operations.[99] The pedagogical and sociological aspects are included in the approaches of organizational theory. The analyses of approaches using organizational theory focus on the findings of the literature analyses about Auftragstaktik, which gives references to elements of organizational theories (see Appendix 1) like self-regulation, system theory, decentralization and delegation, principal-agent theory, concept of heterarchy and network theory.

The selected approaches using organizational theory, which support the understanding of Auftragstaktik as a comprehensive leadership and management concept, measure performance and effectiveness on several levels: individual, group and institutional/organizational level. They can be addressed to subordinates, superiors, peers and further stakeholders and they can be fixed to each of these levels as follows (see Table 3.1). Auftragstaktik as a leadership concept could be assessed by the leadership functions "Leading the people" (individual/group) and

---

[98] Oetting, Das Chaos beherrschen …, 351. English, The Operational Art …, 5.
[99] See paragraph 3.9.

"Leading the institution" (organization/institution). The selected organizational theoretical approaches show relevant aspects of Auftragstaktik as a management concept and the strong interplay between leadership and management functions.

Table 3.1 – Applied organizational theoretical approaches

level of performance/effectiveness	organizational theoretical approach	addressee
individual	self-regulation	subordinate
group	decentralization, delegation, principal-agent-theory	superior, subordinate
organization/institution	system theory, concept of heterarchy, network theory	superior, subordinate, peers, further stakeholders

3.2 Self-regulation

The concept of self-regulation is important for the understanding of Auftragstaktik and underlines especially the relevance of autonomy, self-initiative, improvisation, participation and learning[100]. Originally, self-regulation is used in system theory and means the achieving of equilibrium through negative or positive feedback. In psychology, self-regulation is a state of behavior characterized by mental balancing without external instruction. Ungerer underlines that self-regulation is prerequisite of Auftrag-

---

[100] The model of self-regulation is comparable to a pedagogical framework of action. Curcio, Auftragstaktik …, 10.

staktik. In contrast, external control is a characteristic of Befehlstaktik (see Figure 3.1).[101]

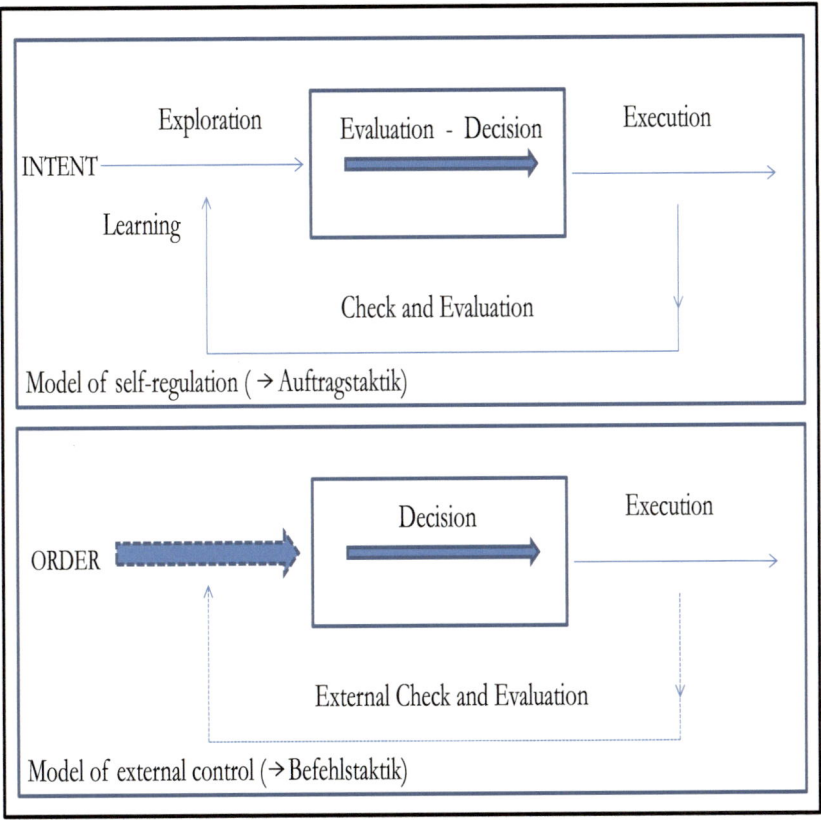

Figure 3.1 - **Model of self-regulation versus model of external control**

Source: Own figure following Dietrich Ungerer, Der militärische Einsatz:172-173.

---

[101] Ungerer, *Der militärische Einsatz* …, 172-173.

3.3 Decentralization and Delegation

Several authors point out that Auftragstaktik is a decentralized command method. Eckart underlines that task-oriented command would be the better term as Auftragstaktik, because, due to division of work, the subordinate takes over the responsibility for the workload under the supervision of his superior in a hierarchical system. In an egalitarian system like a heterarchy[102], the supervision would be mutual between the participants of the heterarchical structure. Eckart formulates the tenets of delegation also for the Auftragstaktik:[103]

- task and responsibility exclusively at the subordinated, delegated level
- a changing situation allows the subordinate to change the task execution
- supervision of the superior should not be misused by active intervention in the task execution (micromanagement)

3.4 Principal-Agent-Theory

The principal-agent-theory[104] is also a useful theory to improve the understanding of Auftragstaktik and to recognize the relevance of trust and responsibility to achieve common goals and

---

[102] See paragraph 3.6.
[103] Eckart, Auftragstaktik zwischen Delegation und Mandat ..., 24.
[104] Bernd Kaluza, Herwig Dullnig, Franz Malle, "Principal-Agent-Probleme in der Supply Chain – Problemanalyse und Diskussion von Lösungsvorschlägen," in *Discussion Paper of the College of Business Administration, University of Klagenfurt*, (Klagenfurt/Austria: Klagenfurt University Press, 2003), 17-20. Sowers uses principal-agent theory to analyse the interplay between soldiers and multiple principals in the new operating environment. Thomas S. Sowers, "Beyond the Soldier and the State: Contemporary Operations and Variance in Principle-Agent Relationships," *Armed Forces & Society*, no. 3, (Spring 2005): 385-386.

maximise total utility under conditions of information asymmetry. The problem of motivating a party to act on behalf of another is known as 'the principal–agent problem'. The principal–agent problem arises when a principal has to compensate an agent for performing certain acts that are useful to the principal and costly to the agent. The principal has difficulties to observe the agent's performance because of information asymmetries. Similar situations can also occur in military "principal-agent-relationships" suffering information asymmetry, uncertainty and risk. The subordinate and the superior are maximising and prioritising their individual utilities (see Figure 3.2 – case I). The relation between superior and subordinate are marked by information asymmetry, which grants the subordinate an information advantage. Auftragstaktik means that the individual utility is aligned with the common intent of the superior (see Figure 3.2 - case II). Both sides are focussed on the common intent. In the case of asymmetric information, the subordinate acts independently and his incentive is to achieve the common intent of the superior. Auftragstaktik bridges the problem in such way that the superior grants the subordinate freedom of action. This autonomy of action is a compensation for the subordinate to act according to the common intent of the superior. The maximising of participation nurtures self-confidence and self-satisfaction, which develops intrinsic motivation. Auftragstaktik solves this principal-agent-problem through its focus on fair cooperation between superior and subordinate based on mutual trust. This contract of trust reduces transaction costs significantly.

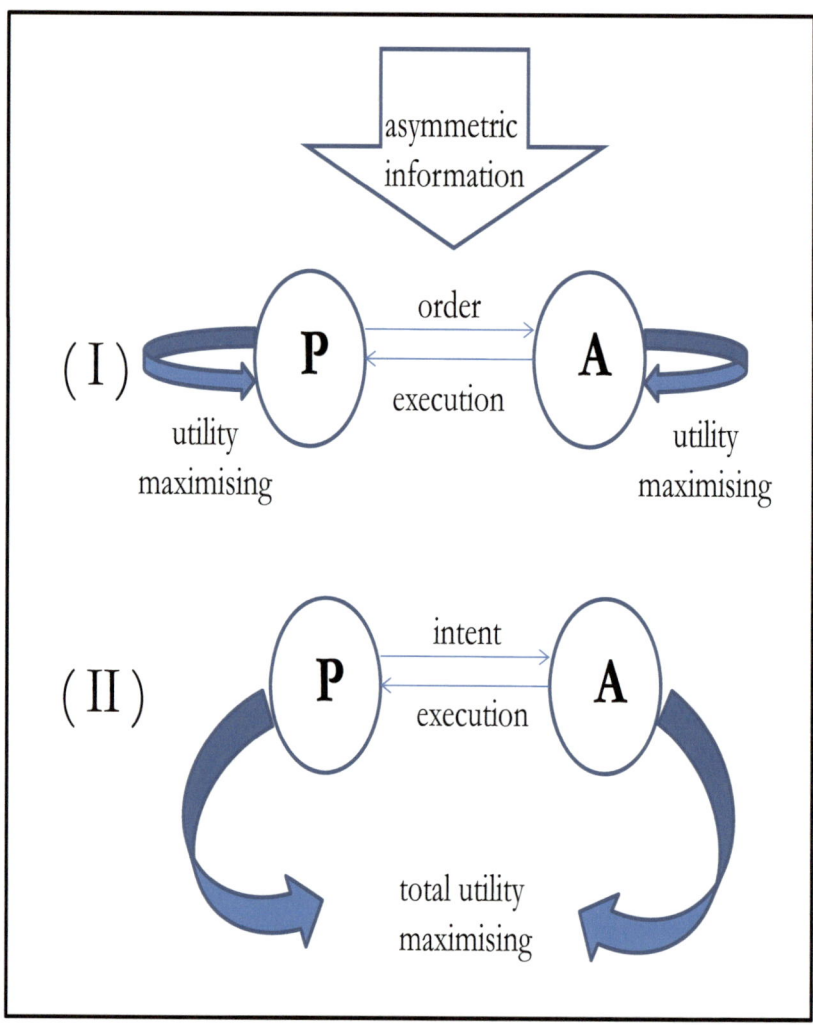

Figure 3.2 - Principal-Agent relation and utility maximising
Source: Own figure following Jochen Wittmann, "Leadership und Heterarchie": 19.

3.5 System Theory by Luhmann

Luhmann's social theory[105] delivers a valuable basic for the understanding of Auftragstaktik. Keller refers to Luhmann's social system theory in context to his definition of Auftragstaktik as method to reduce complexity, which underlines especially the importance of freedom of action, participation, trust, self-initiative and self-regulation.[106] The main element of Luhmann's social system theory is communication. The system according to Luhmann exists within an environment, which is also called super-system. The input- and output-relations between the system and its super-system are system-relevant. The system transfers the given input by transformation or interpretation into an output. There is a differentiation between trivial and non-trivial machines.[107] Trivial machines just transfer the input into output. Non-trivial machines are able to transfer the input according to interpretation into an output, which is non-determinable. They cover human beings, groups of human beings and human societies.

The transformation/interpretation operates by selecting only a limited amount of data available outside. The processing of meaning transfers the data into information by reduction of complexity. Social systems are therefore systems of communication, which possess their own, unique identity. The social systems have the opportunity to adapt themselves better to their environments. Furthermore, Luhmann differentiates between *Zweckprogrammierung* (programming of goals) and *Konditionalprogrammierung* (programming of conditions). The *Zweckprogram-*

---

[105] Niklas Luhmann, *Social Systems*, translated by John Bednarz Jr., (Stanford: Stanford University Press, 1995): 1-2.
[106] Keller, Mythos Auftragstaktik ..., 142.
[107] Heinz von Foerster, *Sicht und Einsicht*, (Braunschweig: Carl-Auer-Verlag, 1985), 12.

mierung means to manage complexity by meaning and *Konditionalprogrammierung* embodies the management of complexity by rules,[108] which is often executed by bureaucracies with the Befehlstaktik. Keller argues that Auftragstaktik is a form of coordination of a system based on non-trivial machines, which is comparable with Luhmann's *Zweckprogrammierung*.[109] Another important element of Luhmann's theory is trust, which he defined as a mechanism for reducing social complexity.[110] Trust between the superiors and their subordinates is a *conditio sine qua non* of Auftragstaktik. Trust supports the transformation of input into output of a system with non-trivial machines (see Figure 3.3).

The environments can vary between different scenarios of contemporary conflicts. The commander's higher intent is the scheduled output, whose requirements are met by the system through interpretation of the available resources. The system, e.g. a tactical or operational unit, is therefore able to flexibly respond to changing requirements in order to achieve the mission success covered by the commander's higher intent.

Luhmann's theory is a capable approach to explain the application of Auftragstaktik, which is focused on leadership and management of complexity, and its effectiveness in a fluid environment.

---

[108] Luhmann, *Social Systems*, 202-203.
[109] Keller, Mythos Auftragstaktik …, 144.
[110] Niklas Luhmann, *Vertrauen: Ein Mechanismus zur Reduktion sozialer Komplexität*, 4th ed. (Stuttgart: Lucius & Lucius, 2000): 27.

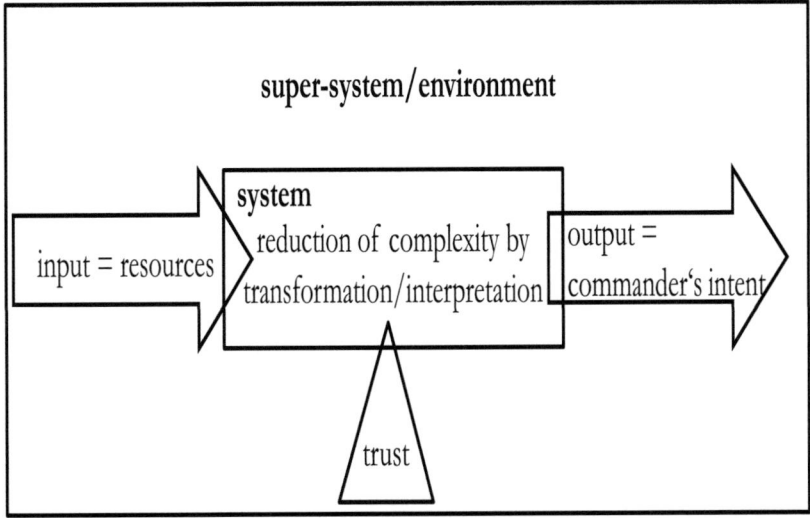

Figure 3.3 - Auftragstaktik in context of Luhmann's theory
Source: Own figure following Jörg Keller, "Mythos Auftragstaktik": 143.

3.6 Concept of Heterarchy

Several authors mention the non-hierarchical character of Auftragstaktik, e.g. in context with emergent leadership or "horizontal team spirit", which raise the question about non-hierarchical concepts of organizations.[111] Such a concept of organizational theory within the complexity science is the concept of heterarchy. Once, McCulloch introduced this term from the subject of neurobiology,[112] but recently mostly applied in economy and business

---

[111] Oetting, Das Chaos beherrschen ..., 349. "Nothing laid down from above in advance is sacrosanct." Richard E. Simpkin, "Command from the Bottom," *Infantry*, (March/April 1985): 34, 35.

[112] Warren McCulloch, "A Heterarchy of Values Determined by the Topology of Nervous Nets", *Bulletin of Mathematical Biophysics*, vol. 7, (1945): 89-93.

science. This concept is related to the delegation concept, but uses a much wider framework.

In the following, two definitions of heterarchy are relevant for further analyses. Reihlen defines heterarchy as a self-regulating organisation, which is able to orient its common patterns to classify to conditions and requirements of the problems to be solved and replaces fix hierarchical structures with a flexible model of temporarily not fixed as well as with closely autonomous and independent actors.[113] Bellmann considers heterarchy as principle of fluctuating hierarchical relations, which could change situational and context-related.[114] Heterarchy is therefore a form of coordination and not a form of organisation, as Reihlen proposed. This means, for example, in heterarchies that hierarchical relations can temporarily go into reverse, which is often caused by an information or/and knowledge advantage of the originally subordinate person/unit. The following table shows the core discriminating characteristics between hierarchy and heterarchy, which should provide more clarity about the terms (see Table 3.2):

---

[113] Markus Reihlen, "Führung in Heterarchien", *Arbeitsbericht Nr. 98 des Seminars für Allgemeine Betriebswirtschaftslehre, Betriebswirtschaftliche Planung und Logistik der Universität Köln* (1998): 11.
[114] Klaus Bellmann, "Heterarchische Produktionsnetzwerke – ein konstruktivistischer Ansatz", in *Kooperations- und Netzwerkmanagement*, ed. by Klaus Bellmann, 31-54, (Berlin: Duncker & Humblot, 2001): 38.

Table 3.2 - Differentiation between hierarchy and heterarchy as forms of coordination

hierarchy	heterarchy
principle of instruction	interaction principle
monocentric organisation	polycentric organisation (network)
vertical informaton /communication	horizontal information /communication
one-sided dependency	interactive, reciprocal dependency
unilateral decision process	cooperative decision process
exclusion of participation	maximizing of participation
autocratic decision-making	democratic decision-making

Source: Own Table following Markus Reihlen, "Führung …": 11-16.

There are specific effects of heterarchy, which include augmented transparency in the decision process, accessibility of information (sources), fair conflict solving mechanism, dependency on initiative and self-responsibility of the participants, use of decentralized knowledge, maximizing of opportunities of participation and the use of democratic decision-making procedures.[115]

There are many advantages of heterarchy, which are also useful for the application of Auftragstaktik:

- Autonomy and self-control are important requirements of people acting within heterarchical processes.

---

[115] Reihlen, Führung in Heterarchien …, 11-16.

- The exploitation of leeway through initiative, curiosity, improvisation and research intent as well as commonly agreed tenets like openness, tolerance, honesty and comradeship are essential advantages of heterarchy.
- The creation of an organization based on mutual trust.
- The reduction of transaction costs (supporting the minimax principle).
- The high ability to learn (from each other) within heterarchical processes.

Disadvantages of a heterarchy could arise from:
- A high number of participants, which makes the decision-making process more difficult or impossible and longsome.
- A high and costly level of necessary qualifications and capabilities.
- A high level of intrinsic motivation of the participants.
- The temporary and fluctuant state of heterarchy.[116]

How could the concept of heterarchy be linked to Auftragstaktik, especially understood as a comprehensive leadership and management concept? There are several parallels of characteristics, but it is necessary to have a look at the decision-making and leadership process of heterarchy.

The temporary and fluctuant state of heterarchy makes a remaining hierarchical framework for action necessary. Blecker et al. postulate an overarching planning for their decentralized and autonomous production systems in order to efficiently coordinate

---

[116] Ibid., 11-16.

the bottom-up performances of the production sub-systems. They talk about the so-called "hierarchical heterarchy". The hierarchical elements of this form of coordination are responsible for the framework, in which heterarchical operations are coordinated and adjusted to a common overarching goal.[117] Hejl focuses on the temporary nature of heterarchy and speaks about "temporary hierarchy", which means that heterarchy is embedded in a hierarchical basic coordination.[118] Wittmann refers to processes in the automotive industry, where a focal decision-making unit coordinates heterarchic actions, like supplier innovations of modules, in order to design and build a complex vehicle. He calls this phenomenon "quasi-heterarchy".[119]

Leadership in context of heterarchy is differently shaped than in a hierarchy. The monocentric character of a hierarchy with its requirement of permanent unity in command is not representative for a heterarchy. The unity of command is considered as an ideal principle and must be pragmatically adapted to bottom-up processes of heterarchical activities. Keithly refers this ideal principle to coalition warfare issues,[120] but it is also valuable for heterarchical processes.

The leadership of heterarchies is conducted by experts, who are situational or context-related chosen by the participants and have an information, competence or knowledge advantage,

---

[117] Thorsten Blecker, Bernd Kaluza, "Heterarchische Hierarchie: Ein Organisationsprinzip flexibler Produktionssysteme", in *Discussion Paper of the College of Business Administration, University of Klagenfurt*, (Klagenfurt/Austria: Klagenfurt University Press, 2004), 13.
[118] Peter M. Hejl, "Politik, Pluralismus und gesellschaftliche Selbstregelung", in *Politische Steuerung. Steuerbarkeit und Steuerungsfähigkeit. Beiträge zur Grundlagendiskussion,* ed. by Heinrich Busshoff, (Baden-Baden: Nomos, 1992): 129.
[119] Jochen Wittmann, *Target Project Budgeting,* (Wiesbaden: Deutscher Universitäts-Verlag, 1998): 233.
[120] Keithly, Auftragstaktik ..., 128-129.

which leads to an information asymmetry and could be used/exploited for superior leadership. In military terms, the subordinate leader can be considered as an expert, because he has the situational awareness and information. If leadership is defined as personal influence on another individual or group focusing on a commonly agreed aim[121], then heterarchical leadership could only be effective if an overarching principle exists. Realistically, the heterarchical leadership must be aligned e.g. with the organizations' strategy or common intent, which is to be an overarching aim. This is necessary to orchestrate the heterarchical activities on the tactical, operational and strategic level. In heterarchies, the common intent (or aim or strategy) replaces temporarily the unity of command in classical hierarchies. In the military context, subordinates are explicitly allowed to act independently situational or context-related on behalf of the common intent. In this case, they act as experts because of their specific knowledge of the situation or context. In contrary to classical heterarchy, they are not chosen by their comrades and supporting units within the heterarchy. In the quasi-heterarchy the subordinates act as experts with a temporary different role in the military organization. Nevertheless, main elements of heterarchy are vital for functioning of heterarchical situations in military operations. Therefore, a quasi-heterarchy (heterarchical hierarchy) is a possible form of coordination in context of the application of Auftragstaktik. This is relevant in the cases where the situation completely changed for the subordinate or a completely new situation occurs, which is not covered by the implied tasks of the order. Heterarchical elements in the decision-making process have impacts on strategic thinking, strategy formulation, monitoring and controlling. This has

---

[121] Ulrich, *Management …,* 139.

also implications on the quality of the institution and questions the ability to innovate and to change for the military institution.[122]

Democratic decision-making processes as part of leadership and management processes are common in different environments using the term of system theory. Democratic decision making has four characteristics, the ballot, the compromise, the consensus and the expert's decision.[123] These characteristics can be linked to different environments (see Figure 3.4).

The military system applying Auftragstaktik can also be involved in these considerations. The subordinate receives the position of an expert, because of his situational information advantage and the action outside the assigned tasks of the order in case of a dramatic change of situation (see Figure 3.5).[124]

---

[122] Schmidtchen, *The Rise of the Strategic Private ...*, 304, 306.
[123] Reihlen, Führung in Heterarchien ..., 33.
[124] An established general principle of the soldier to act independently and autonomously based on ethical values is very helpful, e.g. the concept of *Innere Führung*. Claus von Rosen, "Die ZDv 10/1 Innere Führung von 2008. Vorschrift - Handbuch - Überbau," in *Jahrbuch Innere Führung 2009*, ed. by Uwe Hartmann et al., 17-51, (Eschede: miles-Verlag, 2009), 23.

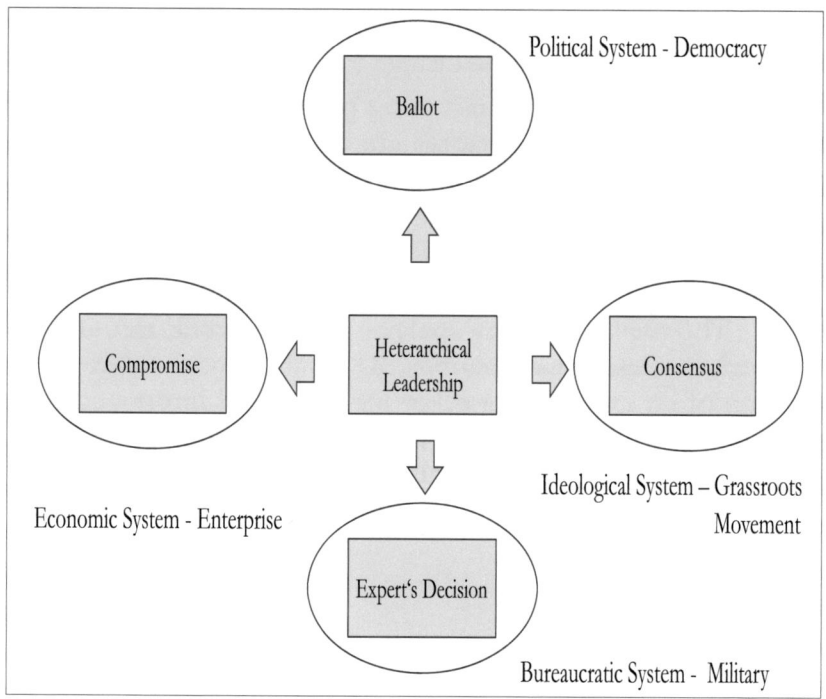

Figure 3.4 - **Heterarchical leadership through democratic decision-making process in different systems**

Source: Own figure following Jochen Wittmann, "Leadership und Heterarchie": 12.

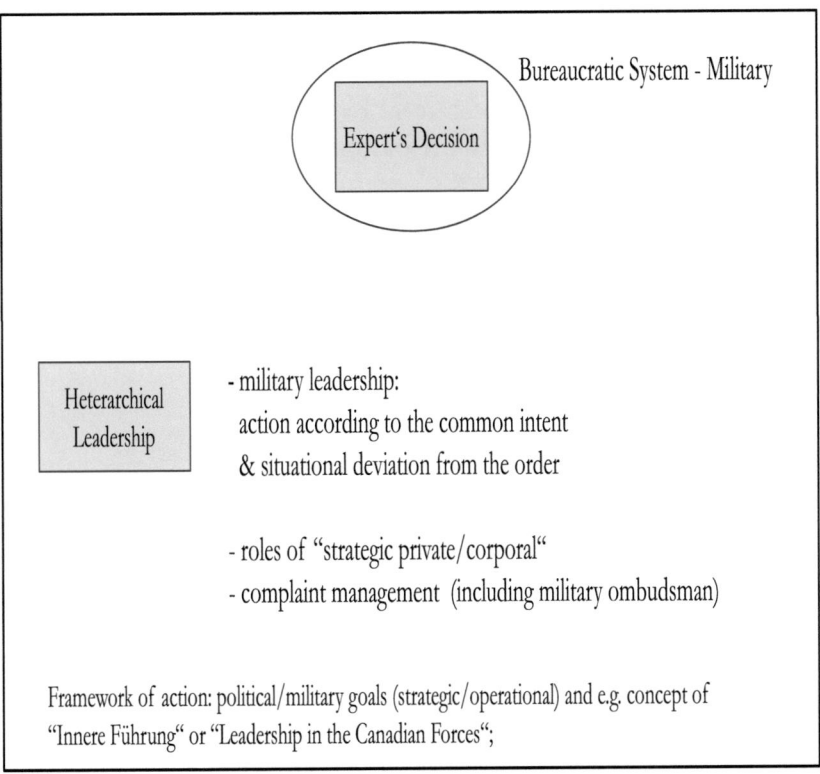

Figure 3.5 - Heterarchical leadership in a military organisation applying Auftragstaktik

Source: Own figure following Jochen Wittmann, "Leadership und Heterarchie": 12.

Heterarchy also influences the strategy (building) process of the (military) institution, which is based on the consideration that tactical actions can have a strategic impact. Bellmann underlines the different characteristics of strategies between hierarchy and heterarchy. The application of Auftragstaktik in a quasi-heterarchical environment leads to a "strategy as concerted sublimate", which is achieved by coordination through common intent (see Table 3.3).

The concept of heterarchy backs insights of Moltke the Elder, that strategy is a system of operational actions and reactions (*Aushilfen*). This comes close to the strategy as concerted sublimate of a quasi-heterarchical process. Activities of decentralized subordinate commanders could be aggregated to strategy according to the common intent. Moltke the Elder underlined the relevance of updating the strategic plan during operations and the possibility that

> a victory won without – or even against – higher orders can still be part of the totality, for each victory carries with it far-reaching effects. The commander will add it into his calculations, as he does all those other facts that went into modifying the plan he originally conceived and held to steadily.[125]

---

[125] Helmuth von Moltke , in Bigge, *Ueber Selbstthätigkeit der Unterführer ...*, 308.

Table 3.3 - Types of strategy with different forms of coordination[126]

type of strategy	strategy as plan	strategy as sublimate	strategy as concerted sublimate
form of coordination	hierarchy	heterarchy	quasi-heterarchy
aim of control	accomplishment of task	result orientation	mission accomplishment
principle of control	direct control	indirect control	indirect control
variable of control	command of management	pattern of action of participants	pattern of action according to common intent
direction of control	top-down	bottom-up	top-down/bottom-up
dynamics of control	periodical	repetitive	repetitive, ad-hoc
activity	execution	exploration, interpretation, interaction	exploration, interpretation, interaction
principle of supervision	centrally	decentrally	decentrally
delegation	no	yes	yes
command system	Befehlstaktik	*Projekt-/Entschlusstaktik*	Auftragstaktik

Source: Own table following Klaus Bellmann, "Heterarchische...": 35.

---

[126] In the case of lacking an overarching goal/intent the command system is called in non-military terms *Projekttaktik* (project tactics) and in military terms *Entschlusstaktik* (resolution tactics), characterizing its temporary and fluctuant character. The commander/soldier acts solely on his own resolution (*Entschluss*).

Moltke also agreed about the temporary and fluctuant nature of ad-hoc activities and updates of the general plan without or against high orders on the subordinates' level, which points out that there temporarily exists a status of quasi-heterarchy. Critics of Auftragstaktik like Naveh and Geyer emphasized the lacking of a coherent strategy, because according to Naveh it was just an avalanche of actions that exploited success by tactical success and not by design[127] and Geyer stated this flood of action was squeezed into something it never was: an operational design.[128]

Maybe, both critics lacked the understanding of the temporary heterarchical nature in war, which was characterized by uncertainty and chaos, as Moltke has recognized.

The question is how to construct a strategy as concerted sublimate? This means that the core information for strategy formulation or adaption results from bottom-up information. For example, the rise of grass-root developments, like insurgency movements or terrorist networks like Al-Qaeda with political goals and global reach[129], can cause a strategy change during peace operations. The concept of heterarchy allows insights into the application of Auftragstaktik in fluid environments and underlines that Auftragstaktik covers leadership and management issues, also under heterarchical conditions. It also shows the bottom-up impacts to strategy building, as Moltke recognized.

---

[127] Shimon Naveh, *In Pursuit of Military Excellence: The Evolution of Operational Theory*, (London: Frank Cass, 1997), 121.

[128] Michael Geyer, "German Strategy in the Age of Machine Warfare, 1914-45", in *Makers of Modern Strategy* ed. by Peter Paret, 527-597, (Princeton: Princeton University Press, 1986): 586.

[129] Kinross, Clausewitz ..., 45-46.

3.7 Network Theory

The network theory[130] is a valuable approach to describe the application of Auftragstaktik as well as new forms of organisations within the new operational environment. These are coined by many stakeholders on the non-military side (governmental, constabulary, civil, NGO) as well as on the military side, because military and political coalitions are more the rule than the exception. Another aspect is the effective use of new technology in the new operating environment, which is often summarized as "network-centric warfare"[131] or "network enabled capability"[132] and recognized as Revolution in Military Affairs. In general, RMA contains four elements: technological change, systems development, operational innovation and institutional adaptation.[133] The network theory plays a vital role in economic and business science and is well-developed. Therefore, the theoretical foundation should be transferred to the military science. The following definition is the starting point for further analyses:

A network is a form of economic organisation between market and hierarchy, which is characterised by the realisation of competitive advantages and a polycentric structure, and is strategically led by one or more enterprises. The chiefly stable relations

---

[130] In general, network theory has an intraorganizational as well as an interorganizational focus. An intraorganizational network could be a joint task force of national armed forces. The focus in this study lies on interorganizational networks.
[131] Shilling, Enabling Organizational Innovation …, n.p.
[132] United Kingdom MoD, "NEC Network Enabled Capability", *Information Warfare Site*, (2003), http://www.iwar.org.uk/rma/resources/uk-mod/nec.htm#doc, accessed August 4, 2010.
[133] Colin S. Gray, *Strategy for chaos: revolutions in military affairs and the evidence of history*, (London: Cass, 2002): 120.

within the network of independent enterprises are marked more by cooperation and reciprocity than by competition.[134]

If an armed conflict is a synonym for the free use of lethal forces, it could be considered as operating environment for the military, which is in analogy comparable with the market synonym for free competitive conditions.

In the terminology of heterarchy, there are different forms of coordination like hierarchy, heterarchy as well as market and conflict (see Table 3.3). The definition of networks for a military or security-creating environment could be the following:

A network is a form of organisation between armed conflict and hierarchy, which is characterised by the realisation of security (and stability) advantages and a polycentric structure, and is led by one or more institutions. The chiefly stable relations within the network of independent organisations are marked more by cooperation and reciprocity than by competition.

Eckart points out in context to the application of Auftragstaktik, that there are differences between individual and collective systems. He underlines that (business) networks are generally individual systems based on legal transactions in contrast to a military organisation with Auftragstaktik as command system, which focuses on a common overarching intent for efficient co-ordination.[135]

The definition of network in the military context has to assume a collective system character, especially within a coalition or alliance. In practise, the network of a peace support operation includes a hybrid form of individual systems (NGOs) and collective systems (military coalitions). It is necessary to assume in this

---

[134] Jörg Sydow, *Strategische Netzwerke: Evolution und Organisation*, (Wiesbaden: Gabler, 1993): 82.
[135] Eckart, Auftragstaktik zwischen Delegation und Mandat ..., 24.

case, that it is possible to agree on an overarching goal within this hybrid network as core coordination frame. One of the core characteristics of a network is the existence of a minimum of one focal institution leading the network.

This focal institution influences the level of involvement to the armed conflict and the access to the required resources, which is mainly organised through the shaping of interaction within the network. The focal institution could use directives or guidelines to control or influence the network partners. In terms of Auftragstaktik the commander's intent could receive the overarching function of combining the network partners on a common goal.

The picture of a network becomes clearer in examples like warfighting of a coalition or peace support operations where military, constabulary, governmental and non-governmental institutions are participating and interlinked to create security as well as stability. The network of a peace support operation could be organised as follows: The UN could be the focal institution for coordinating the international NGO, the government of the failed state could be the focal institution of local military, police and other GO and the NATO could be the focal institution of the international/coalition military units. Network theory is able to explain the structure and processes of conditions of the contemporary military environment, e.g. peace operations, where Auftragstaktik plays an exceptional role through management and leadership characteristics. This influences and shapes military institutions, too.

3.8 Synopsis of relevant approaches

Each organizational theoretical approach could be linked to relevant characteristics of Auftragstaktik. The approaches are addressed to the participants of leadership processes as well as to the different levels of performance and command (see Table 3.4). The relevance of the approaches to these topics could be underlined and analyzed. The usability of organizational approaches to explain Auftragstaktik as a comprehensive and effective leadership and management concept is supported. It also reveals that Auftragstaktik is able to influence all levels of command and levels of performance. Therefore, Auftragstaktik has a much broader perspective and reach as a pure command technique on the tactical and operational level. It covers functions, e.g. trust and learning effect, which have strong impacts on management and leadership functions of the institution as well, which was especially underlined in combination with the concept of heterarchy and network theory. The network theory gives also an interesting approach to explain the contemporary military environment, which requires the application of Auftragstaktik as a comprehensive leadership and management concept. Hence, this makes Auftragstaktik a core competence of mastering the military operational art (see Table 3.4).

Table 3.4 - Synopsis of relevant approaches[136]

requirements of Auftragstaktik	self-regulation	decentra-lization/ delegation	principal-agent-theory	system theory	concept of heterarchy	network theory	level of command & conflict			level of performance & effectiveness		
							tactical	operational	strategic	individual	group	institution
decentralization		x	x	x	x	x	x	x		x	x	
delegation		x	x	x	x	x	x	x		x	x	
freedom of action	x	x	x	x	x	x	x	x		x	x	
cost-benefit-ratio		x	x	x	x	x	x	x	x	x	x	x
bottom-up-orientation/participation	x	x	x	x	x	x	x	x		x	x	
learning effect	x	x	x	x	x	x	x	x	(x)	x	x	(x)
trust (reciprocity)		x		x	x	x	x	x	x	x	x	x
self-initiative	x	x	x	x	x	x	x	x		x	x	
self-regulation	x			x	x		x	x		x		
flexibility	x	x		x	x	x	x	x	(x)	x	x	(x)
intrinsic responsibility	x	x		x	x	x	x			x		
creativity/improvisation	x	x		x	x	x	x	x	(x)	x	x	(x)
speed of decision-making		x				x	x	x	x	x	x	x
details of order							x	x	x	x	x	x

---

[136] Legend: x relevant; (x) partly relevant.

The reduction of complexity and the flexibility to adapt to changing situations represent Auftragstaktik's strength, which is underlined by several approaches of the organizational theory (see Figure 3.6).

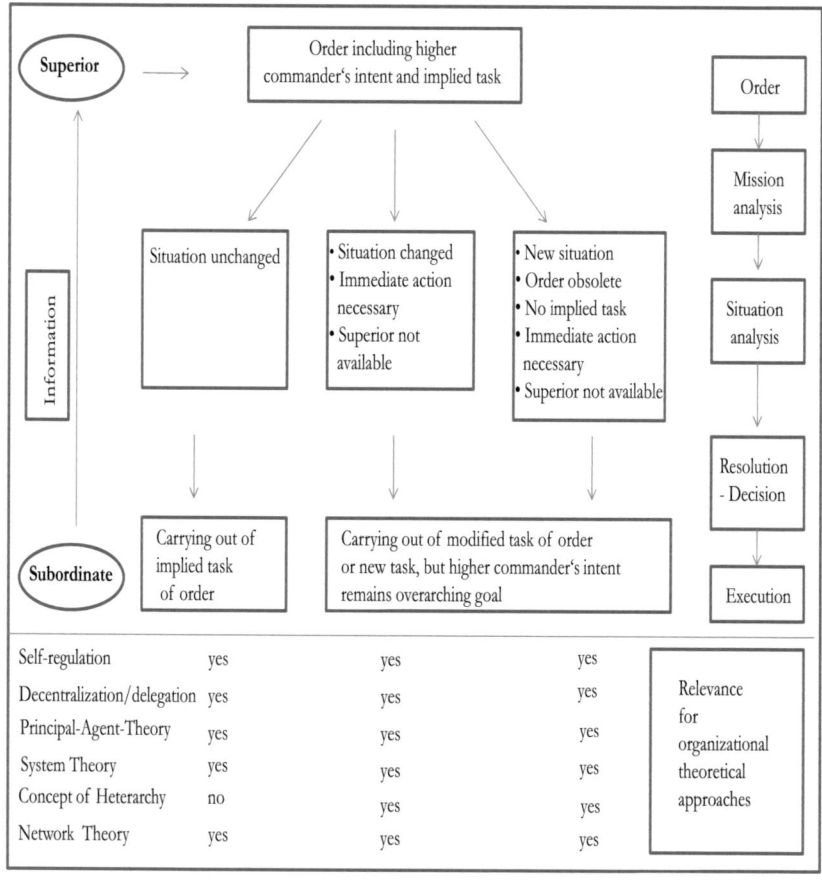

Figure 3.6 - Cases of applying Auftragstaktik

3.9 Auftragstaktik as a comprehensive leadership and management concept for the contemporary military environment

Auftragstaktik understood as a comprehensive leadership and management concept includes all levels of command and conflict. The question is, is it possible to apply Auftragstaktik as a comprehensive leadership and management concept in the contemporary military environment?

In the following, a case of complex peace operation is presented to exemplify the Auftragstaktik as a comprehensive leadership and management concept.

The complex peace operation is characterized by a wide range of military and non-military actors and has the establishing of security and stability in the relevant area as overarching goal. The focal players on the strategic level could be a coalition of countries engaging in peace operation in a fragile state, the United Nations, which coordinate the NGOs in the fragile state, and the government of the fragile state with its GOs and security organizations. On the operational level, there could be the coalition's military headquarters in the fragile state, the UN representation office and NGO country headquarters and the national military and police headquarters. The tactical level is represented by the coalition's provincial reconstruction team and its units, the NGO working teams on the provincial and local level and finally the local military and police headquarters.

Pending on the level of violence or the threat of violence, the military tasks on the operational and tactical level vary between tasks with constabulary (non-combat) character, like mobile and stationary checkpoints, and with classical military (combat) character, like counter-insurgency activities.

The strategic military level of each participating nation defines its ROEs, which reflect core interests and are additional requirements included in the orders. Based on the system view, the ROE are in general aligned with Auftragstaktik,[137] because they belong to the environment of the system, e.g. tactical or operational commander has to adapt to. Despite of this, it is necessary to organize the ROE modification and monitoring process flexible and quick in order to adapt to changing environments as soon as possible. The criminal law and other regulations except the LOAC should not limit the leeway of action and the conduct of Auftragstaktik in the new operating environment.[138]

The use of Befehlstaktik by coalition partners replaces *Zweckprogrammierung* through *Konditionalprogrammierung*, which makes the application of Auftragstaktik impossible.[139] The reason is, that the leeway for interpretation within the system does not exist or is severely limited with Befehlstaktik. Therefore, there must be a clear division of responsibilities in multinational operations between armies with Auftragstaktik and Befehlstaktik.

Bureaucracy caused by rules not adapted to the situation of the peace operation could also handicap the use of Auftragstaktik, but special regulations as well as exceptional rules could solve this problem.

NCW, understood as enabler of complex operation, is welcome for Auftragstaktik, but within a military coalition the technology standards must be equivalent and cooperation and coordination must be possible in order to prevent information asymmetries.[140]

---

[137] Dirk Freudenberg, "Das grundsätzliche Spannungsverhältnis zwischen der Auftragstaktik, Rules of Engagement (ROE) und der deutschen Strafrechtsordnung," *Österreichische Militärische Zeitung*, no. 1, (2006), 51.
[138] Ibid.,51.
[139] Keller, Mythos Auftragstaktik ..., 148.
[140] Paul T. Mitchell, *Network Centric Warfare*, (New York: Routledge, 2006), 43-44.

In the overarching network, Auftragstaktik is a concept to meet the requirements of other players, like NGOs and local GOs, and security and stability in the region.

Auftragstaktik is the relevant system for complex peace operations, because it creates an effective coordination as well as communication and, therefore, a good management and leadership in a fluid environment. The intense involvement of the strategic level in the network makes the strong impact of Auftragstaktik as a stabilizing factor a *conditio sine qua non*. The strategic level can use the bottom-up information for strategy monitoring and as Moltke claimed to update the strategic plan.

As an example, Vogelaar concluded in an empirical analysis about Dutch peace operations, that the less successful peace operation lacked a clear common intent, which led to a failure of the operation. This could be a hint, that the strategy was wrong and had to be updated on situational conditions. A *Zweckprogrammierung* on the strategic level did not take place. This could be prevented, when Auftragstaktik would be applied and bottom-up information accepted on the strategic level for updating the strategic plan.

In this case, the deviation of an order because of a completely changing situation is not only possible during warfighting or peace enforcement operations. It is essential as well as necessary for other peace operations. It also depends on the institution, which must acknowledge change and innovation, especially from bottom-up, and which should not act as a bureaucracy, a form of *Konditionalprogrammierung*.

The mixing of the levels of conflict during OOTW requires more two-way-communication and coordination between the levels of command, which is a core asset of Auftragstaktik. Therefore, the relevance of Auftragstaktik seems to grow as it is a comprehensive management and leadership concept, which creates the basis for effective and efficient coordination within the networks of contemporary military environments coined by specific forms of coordination, like heterarchy and conflict.

The broaden understanding of Auftragstaktik makes it more relevant for OOTWs and underlines the importance of its seemingly timeless tenets, developed by clear-sighted officers more than hundred years ago. They could not count on the support by organizational theories but on their broad experience and common sense, which helped to develop the Auftragstaktik as the core pillar of mastering military operational art.

4   CONCLUSION AND FUTURE RESEARCH

Auftragstaktik is much more than a tactical command technique. The literature analysis considered a broad variety of definitions and concepts. Based on a deep analysis, the Auftragstaktik overarching determinants, tenets and principles could be identified. The organization theory gives explanations to the concept of Auftragstaktik and identifies it as a core competence in management and leadership. Simultaneously, it is a cornerstone of the operational art in the new operating environment that can be underlined by insights especially of systems theory, concept of heterarchy and network theory.

The misunderstanding of "German" operational art could be explained based on new insights of organizational theory. The exploitation of tactical successes instead of operational design is a determinant of the successful application of Auftragstaktik with its deep heterarchic determinants and characteristics. The operational art must adapt these effects, especially in context to OOTW in new operating environment.

The innovative character of Auftragstaktik is especially linked to heterarchic characteristics. In business, the open innovation concept is similar, where bottom-up information and ideas from internal and especially external sources lead to new products and processes, which improve the business model and the business as form of organisation in total.[141] Hippel calls this "democratizing of innovation", which is an effective enabler for institutional change, too.[142] Further research could link this concept with Auftragstaktik and military operational art.

Applied concepts of leadership should also include explicitly heterarchical components in order to adapt Auftragstaktik, because it is a comprehensive management and leadership concept more than a pure command technique. Auftragstaktik is the only capable management and leadership concept to counter frictions effectively in the contemporary military environment and therefore a core pillar for mastering the military operational art.

---

[141] Henry W. Chesborough, "The era of open innovation," *MIT Sloan Management Review*, (Spring 2003): 36-37.
[142] Eric von Hippel, *Democratizing Innovation*, (Cambridge/London: MIT Press, 2006): 13-15.

Appendix 1: Overview of complexity science

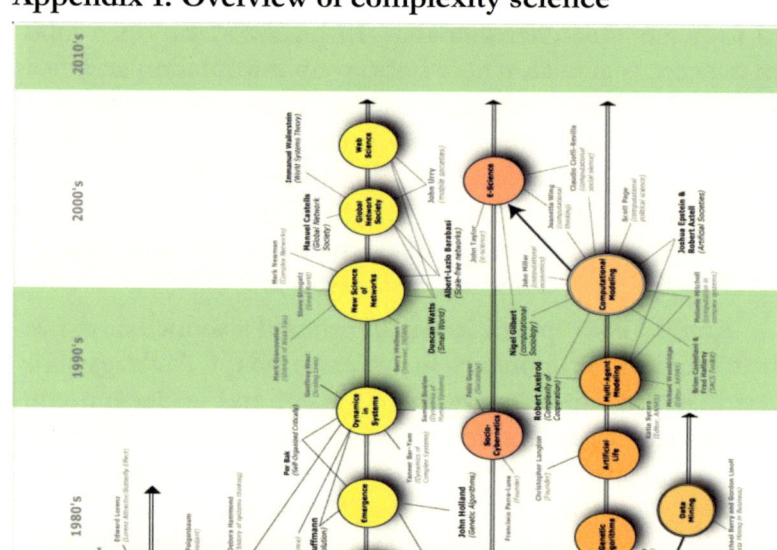

Figure A 1.1: Overview of complexity science

Source: Brian Castellani, Frederic William Hafferty, *Sociology and Complexity Science*, xi.

Appendix 2: Results of Literature Analysis

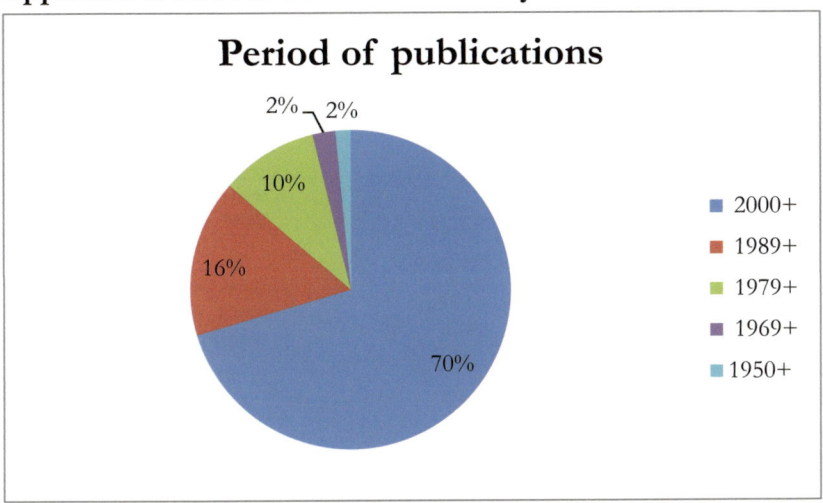

Figure A 2.1: Period of publications about Auftragstaktik
Source: Own analysis (N=132).

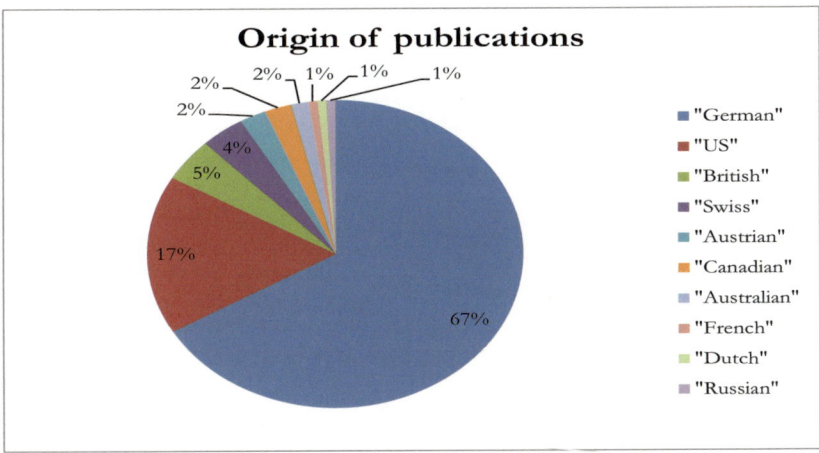

Figure A 2.2: Origin of publications about Auftragstaktik
Source: Own analysis (N=132).

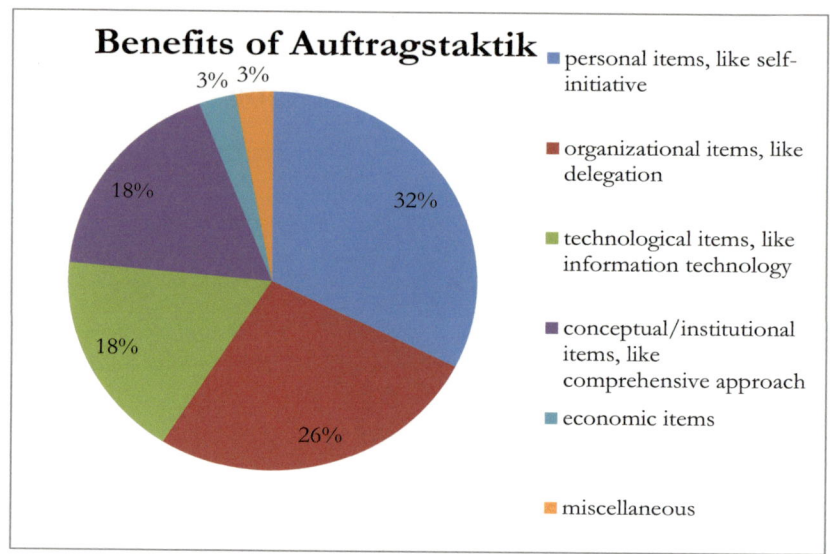

Figure A 2.3: Benefits of Auftragstaktik
Source: Own analysis (N=34, including duplications).

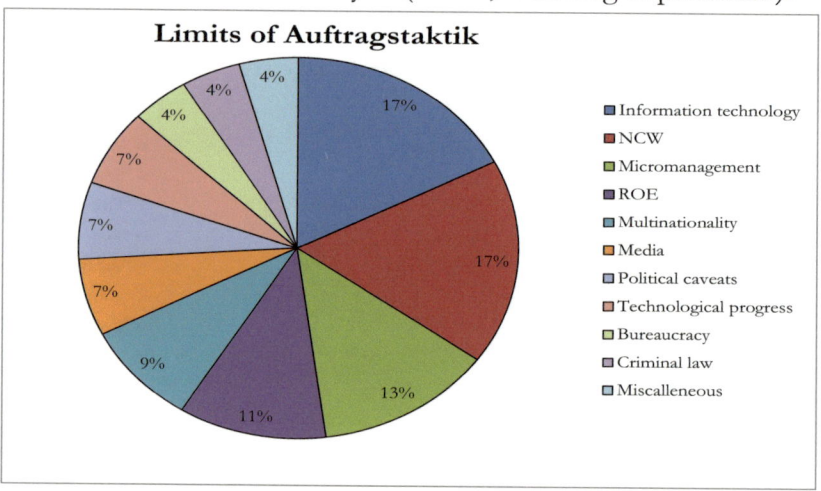

Figure A 2.4: Limits of Auftragstaktik
Source: Own analysis (N=46, including duplications).

BIBLIOGRAPHY

Arnold, Michael. "Auftragstaktik: Entwicklung und Bedeutung eines Führungsverständnisses." *Allgemeine Schweizerische Militärzeitschrift*, no.12, (2003): 11-14.

Bateman, Robert L. "Force XXI and the Death of Auftragstaktik." *Armor*, (January/February 1996): 13-15.

Bellmann, Klaus. "Heterarchische Produktionsnetzwerke – ein konstruktivistischer Ansatz." In *Kooperations- und Netzwerkmanagement*, edited by Klaus Bellmann, 31-54. Berlin: Duncker & Humblot, 2001.

Bismarck, Otto von. *Gedanken und Erinnerungen*. Stuttgart / Berlin: J. G. Cotta'sche Buchhandlung Nachfolger, 1928.

Blecker, Thorsten, Kaluza, Bernd. "Heterarchische Hierarchie: Ein Organisationsprinzip flexibler Produktionssysteme." In *Discussion Paper of the College of Business Administration, University of Klagenfurt*. Klagenfurt/Austria: Klagenfurt University Press, 2004.

Boot, Max. "Beyond the 3-block war." *Armed Forces Journal*, (March 2006); available from http://www.cfr.org/publication/10204/beyond_the_3block_war.html#; Internet; accessed 3 August, 2010.

Bühlmann, Christian, Braun, Peter. "Auftragstaktik in Vergangenheit, Gegenwart und Zukunft." *Military Power Revue der Schweizer Armee*, no.1, (2010): 50-63.

Canada, Department of National Defence. B-GJ-005-300/FP-000 *Canadian Forces Operations*. Ottawa: DND Canada, 2004.

Canada, Department of National Defence, B-GJ-005-307/FP-030 *Peace Support Operations*. Ottawa: DND Canada, 2002.

Canadian Defence Academy. *Leadership in the Canadian Forces: Conceptual Foundation*. Ottawa: Canadian Forces Leadership Institute, 2005.

Castellani, Brian, Hafferty, Frederic William. *Sociology and Complexity Science*. Berlin/Heidelberg: Springer, 2009, xi, available from http://www.springerlink.com/content/978-3-540-88461-3#section=383920&page=10&locus=7; Internet; accessed 22 August 2010.

Chesborough, Henry W. "The era of open innovation." *MIT Sloan Management Review*, (Spring 2003): 35-41.

Citino, Robert M. *The German Way of War*. Lawrence: University Press of Kansas, 2005.

Clausewitz, Carl von. *Vom Kriege*. 18th edition, Reinbek: Rowohlt Taschenbuch Verlag, 2010.

Collins, Joseph J. "Afghanistan: Winning a Three Block War." *Journal of Conflict Studies*, No. 2, (Winter 2004), 1-16.

Connor, William M. " Emerging Army Doctrine: Command and Control." *Military Review*, (March/April 2002): 80-84.

Creveld, Martin van. "Conclusions: Reflections on Command." In *Command in War*, 261-275, London: Harvard University Press, 1985.

Creveld, Martin van. "Introduction: On Command." In *Command in War*, 1-16, London: Harvard University Press, 1985.

Cullens, J.A.S. "The Realm of Uncertainty: Directive Control and the Modern Battlefield." *Australian Defence Force Journal*, no. 90, September/October 1991: 13-25.

Curcio, Gian-Paolo. "Auftragstaktik im Licht einer pädagogischen Handlungsstruktur." *Allgemeine Schweizerische Militärzeitschrift*, no.12, (2004): 10-11.

Davis, R. R. "Helmuth von Moltke and the Prussian-German Development of a Decentralized Style of Command: Metz and Sedan 1870." *Defence Studies*, no. 1 (March 2005): 83-95.

Durch, William. *UN Peacekeeping, American Politics and the Uncivil Wars of 1990s*, New York: St. Martin's Press, 1998: 8. Quoted in Colin Gerard Magee, *Apples and Oranges: A Comparison of Operational-level Peace Operations Doctrine of Canada, USA and UK*, (master's thesis, US Army Command and General Staff College, 2005), 15.

Echevarria, Antulio J. "Auftragstaktik: In Its Proper Perspective." *Military Review*, (October 1986): 50-56.

Eckhart, Karl. "Auftragstaktik zwischen Delegation und Mandat." *Allgemeine Schweizerische Militärzeitschrift*, no.01/02, (2008): 22-24.

English, Allan. "The Operational Art." In *The Operational Art: Canadian Perspectives – Context and Concepts*, edited by Allan English, et al., 1-74. Kingston, ON: Canadian Defence Academy Press, 2005.

Foerster, Heinz von. *Sicht und Einsicht*. Braunschweig: Carl-Auer-Verlag, 1985.

Foerster, Roland G. "Das operative Denken Moltkes des Älteren und die Folgen." In *Operatives Denken bei Clausewitz, Moltke, Schlieffen und Manstein*, edited by MGFA, 19-42, (Freiburg: Selbstverlag, 1989).

Freudenberg, Dirk. "Das grundsätzliche Spannungsverhältnis zwischen der Auftragstaktik, Rules of Engagement (ROE) und der deutschen Strafrechtsordnung." *Österreichische Militärische Zeitung*, no. 1, (2006): 48-52.

Freudenberg, Dirk. "Der Strategiebegriff bei Clausewitz, Jomini und Erzherzog Karl." In *Jahrbuch 2008 der Clausewitz-Gesellschaft,* edited by Clausewitz-Gesellschaft, 205-215, vol. 4, (Hamburg: Selbstverlag, 2009).

Freudenberg, Dirk. "Die Rezeption deutschen Führungsdenkens im britischen Führungsverständnis unter besonderer Berücksichtigung von 'Auftragstaktik' und 'Innerer Führung'." In *Jahrbuch 2009 der Clausewitz-Gesellschaft,* edited by Clausewitz-Gesellschaft, 268-287, vol. 5, (Hamburg: Selbstverlag, 2009).

Germany, Heeresdienstvorschrift 100/100, "Truppenführung", (Bonn, 15 Oktober 1998).

Geyer, Michael. "German Strategy in the Age of Machine Warfare, 1914-45." In *Makers of Modern Strategy,* edited by Peter Paret, 527-597. Princeton: Princeton University Press, 1986.

Gray, Colin S. *Strategy for chaos: revolutions in military affairs and the evidence of history.* London: Cass, 2002.

Hejl, Peter M. "Politik, Pluralismus und gesellschaftliche Selbstregelung." In *Politische Steuerung. Steuerbarkeit und Steuerungsfähigkeit. Beiträge zur Grundlagendiskussion,* edited by Heinrich Busshoff, 107-142. Baden-Baden: Nomos, 1992.

Hippel, Eric von. *Democratizing Innovation.* Cambridge/London: MIT Press, 2006.

Hughes, Daniel J. "Auftragstaktik." In *International Military and Defense Encyclopedia,* edited by Trevor N. Dupuy, vol. I, New York, 1993: 328-333.

Kaluza, Bernd, Dullnig, Herwig, Malle, Franz. "Principal-Agent-Probleme in der Supply Chain – Problemanalyse und Diskussion von Lösungsvorschlägen." In *Discussion Paper of the College of Business Administration, University of Klagenfurt.* Klagenfurt/Austria: Klagenfurt University Press, 2003.

Keithly, David M., Ferris, Stephen P. "Auftragstaktik, or Directive Control, in Joint and Combined Operations." *Parameters*, no.03, (1999): 118-133.

Kerkemeyer, Frank A. "Auftragstaktik." *Infantry*, no.06 Nov./Dec., (1987): 28-30.

Keller, Jörg. "Mythos Auftragstaktik." In *Armee in der Demokratie: zum Verhältnis von zivilen und militärischen Prinzipien*, edited by Ulrich vom Hagen, 141-163. Wiesbaden: Schriftenreihe des Sozialwissenschaftlichen Instituts der Bundeswehr, 2006.

Kinross, Stuart. "Clausewitz and low-intensity conflict." *The Journal of Strategic Studies*, no. 1 (2004), 35-58.

Kortzfleisch, Gert von. "Militärorganisation." In *Handwörterbuch der Organisation*, edited by Erwin Grochla, (1969): 990-1000.

Krulak, Charles C. "The Strategic Corporal: Leadership in the Three Block War." *Marines Magazine*, January, (1999); available from http://www.au.af.mil/au/awc/awcgate/usmc/strategic_corporal.htm; Internet; 3 August, 2010.

Leistenschneider, Stephan. *Auftragstaktik im preußisch-deutschen Heer 1871-1914.* Hamburg: Mittler, 2002.

Luhmann, Niklas. *Vertrauen: Ein Mechanismus zur Reduktion sozialer Komplexität.* 4th edition, Stuttgart: Lucius & Lucius, 2000.

Luhmann, Niklas. *Social Systems.* Translated by John Bednarz Jr. Stanford: Stanford University Press, 1995.

Matuszek, Krzysztof C. *Der Krieg als autopoetisches System*. Wiesbaden: VS-Verlag für Sozialwissenschaften, 2007.

McCulloch, Warren. "A Heterarchy of Values Determined by the Topology of Nervous Nets." *Bulletin of Mathematical Biophysics*, vol. 7, (1945): 89-93.

Meigs, Montgomery C. "Operational Art in the New Century." *Parameters*, no. 1 (Spring 2001): 1-11.

Meiter, J. S. "Network Enabled Capability: A Theory Desperately in Need of Doctrine. " *Defence Studies*, no. 2 (June 2006): 189-214.

Messerschmidt, Manfred. "Denken auf den Krieg hin." *Militärgeschichte*, no. 2 (2010): 4-7.

Millotat, Christian E. O. *Das preußisch-deutsche Generalstabssystem*. Zürich: vdf-Hochschulverlag, 2000.

Mitchell, Paul T. *Network Centric Warfare*, New York: Routledge, 2006.

Moltke, Helmuth von. In Bigge, Major. *Ueber Selbstthätigkeit der Unterführer im Kriege, Beihefte zum Militär-Wochenblatt*, Berlin: E.S. Mittler, 1894: 17-18. Quoted in Robert M. Citino, *The German Way of War*, (Lawrence: University Press of Kansas, 2005), 308.

Moltke, Helmuth von. In Roger A. Beaumont, *The Nazis' March To Chaos*. Westport: Praeger Publishers, 2000.

Murray, Williamson. *The Making of Strategy: Rulers, States and War*. Cambridge: Cambridge University Press, 1994.

Naveh, Shimon. *In Pursuit of Military Excellence: The Evolution of Operational Theory*. London: Frank Cass, 1997.

O'Brien, M. B. "Directive Control – The Command Panacea?" *Defence Force Journal*, no. 83, (July/August 1990): 2-16.

Oetting, Dirk W. "Das Chaos beherrschen." *Truppenpraxis/Wehrausbildung*, no.5, (2000): 349-355.

Oetting, Dirk W. *Auftragstaktik: Geschichte und Gegenwart einer Führungskonzeption*. Frankfurt / Bonn: Report-Verlag, 1993.

Samuels, Martin. *Command or Control?* London: Frank Cass, 1995.

Palazzo, Albert. *From Moltke To Bin Laden - The Relevance of Doctrine in the Contemporary Military Environment*. Canberra: Land Warfare Studies Centre, 2008. Study Paper on-line; available from http://www.defence.gov.au/army/lwsc/SP315.asp; Internet; accessed 04 July 2010.

Offerdal, Audun, Jacobsen, Jan O. "Auftragstaktik in the Norwegian Armed Forces." *Defense Analysis*, vol.9, no. 2 (1993): 211-223.

Paret, Peter. *Yorck and the era of Prussian reform 1807 -1815*. Princeton: Princeton University Press, 1966.

Peskett, Gordon R. "Levels of War: a new Canadian Model to begin the 21th Century." In *The Operational Art: Canadian Perspectives – Context and Concepts*, edited by Allan English et al., 97-129, (Kingston, ON: Canadian Defence Academy Press, 2005).

Reihlen, Markus. "Führung in Heterarchien." *Arbeitsbericht Nr. 98 des Seminars für Allgemeine Betriebswirtschaftslehre, Betriebswirtschaftliche Planung und Logistik der Universität Köln* (1998).

Rosen, Claus von. "Die ZDv 10/1 Innere Führung von 2008. Vorschrift - Handbuch - Überbau." In *Jahrbuch Innere Führung 2009*, edited by Uwe Hartmann et al., 17-51, (Eschede: miles-Verlag, 2009).

Schmidtchen, David. *The Rise of the Strategic Private: Technology, Control and Change in a Network-Enabled Military.* Duntroon/Australia: Longmedia, 2006.

Shilling, Chris, Slavin, David, Shamir, Eitan, Linkov, Igor. "Enabling Organizational Innovation: Scientific Process and Military Experience." In *C2 for Complex Endeavors* (in press). Command and Control Research Program, US DOD, 2008: n.p.

Silva, John L. "Auftragstaktik: Its Origin and Development." *Infantry*, (September/October 1989): 6-9.

Simpkin, Richard E. "Command from the Bottom." *Infantry*, (March/April 1985): 34-37.

Sowers, Thomas S. "Beyond the Soldier and the State: Contemporary Operations and Variance in Principle-Agent Relationships." *Armed Forces & Society*, no. 3, (Spring 2005): 385-409.

Storr, Jim. "A Command Philosophy for the Information Age: The Continuing Relevance of Mission Command." *Defense Studies* 3, no.3 (Autumn 2003): 119-129.

Sydow, Jörg. *Strategische Netzwerke: Evolution und Organisation.* Wiesbaden: Gabler, 1993.

Taleb, Nassim Nicholas. *The Black Swan: The Impact of the Highly Improbable.* New York: Random House, 2007.

Uhle-Wettler, Franz. "Auftragstaktik." in: *Mars – Jahrbuch für Wehrpolitik und Militärwesen*, no. 1, (1995): 422-437.

Ulrich, Peter, Fluri, Edgar. *Management.* Bern/Stuttgart: Paul Haupt, 1984.

Ungerer, Dietrich. *Der militärische Einsatz.* Potsdam: miles-Verlag, 2003.

United Kingdom MoD. "NEC Network Enabled Capability." *Information Warfare Site*, (2003); available from http://www.iwar.org.uk/rma/resources/uk-mod/nec.htm#doc; Internet; accessed 4 August, 2010.

Vogelaar, Ad L. W., Kramer, Eric-Hans. "Mission Command in Dutch Peace Support Missions." *Armed Forces & Society*, Spring, (2004): 409-431.

Widder, Werner. "Auftragstaktik and Innere Führung: Trademarks of German Leadership." *Military Review*, September-October, (2002): 3-9.

Wittmann, Jochen. "Leadership und Heterarchie: Grundüberlegungen." In: *Forschungsseminar des Center of Market-Oriented Product and Production Management an der Universität Mainz.* Waldbronn: Selbstverlag, 24.07.2010: 1-22.

Wittmann, Jochen. *Target Project Budgeting*. Wiesbaden: Deutscher Universitäts-Verlag, 1998.

Yardley, Ivan. "Crossing the Void, War and Business: Utility of British Military Management Methods Beyond the Military." *Defence Studies* 9, no.1 (March 2009): 5-21.

INDEX

Absicht	40
Afghanistan	27
Al-Qaeda	76
Amorphous war	24
Archduke Charles	21
Aspern, Battle of	21
Asymmetric war/conflict	23, 26
Attrition warfare	21
Auftrag	33, 40
Aushilfen	22, 74
Balkans	27
Befehl	33
Befehls-/Normaltaktik	31, 33, 47, 52, 53, 64, 84
Bismarck	16
Black Swan	20
Blücher	16
British Army	49
Bureaucracy	52, 84, 85
Canadian Forces (College)	30, 34, 43
Canadian Government	26
Caveat	24, 52
Chaos theory	57
Clausewitz	19, 20, 21, 22, 50
Coalition warfare	69
Coalition	77, 78, 83, 84
Cold War	23, 43, 49
Complaint management	73
Complexity science	57, 88
Complexity	15, 17, 19, 24, 29, 38, 44, 50, 51, 52, 55, 63, 64, 65, 82
Concerted sublimate	73, 74, 75, 76
Counter-Insurgency	24, 26, 83
Counter-Terrorism	24
Creveld, van	37, 38, 57
Criminal law	27, 52, 84
Delegation	15, 45, 51, 57, 60, 66
Directive Control	43
Entscheidung	40
Entschlusstaktik	75
EU	27
Field Manual	39, 49
Fog of war	20, 50
Frederick the Great	39
Frictions	20, 50, 87
Führen mit Auftrag	33, 42, 43
Führungsgrundsätze	45

Geneva conventions	23
German Army	5, 6, 21, 29, 39
Gneisenau	16
Golan Heights	27
Grass-root development	72, 76
Grievance system	42
Hegel	39
Hessian Army	39
Heterarchy	15, 57, 60, 65, 78, 80, 86
Heuristic	21, 22
Hierarchical heterarchy	69
Innere Führung	71, 73
Jäger	39
Jena and Auerstedt	39
Jomini	21
Konditionalprogrammierung	63, 64, 84, 85
Krulak	26
Lage	40
LOAC	23, 84
Luhmann	63
Manoeuvre warfare	49
Manstein	45
Micromanagement	17, 29, 52, 60
Millotat	7, 17
Mission Command	43
Mission-oriented Command and Control	5
Mission-type Tactics	43
Moltke the Elder	16, 21, 22, 23, 31, 74, 76, 85
Motivation	35, 50, 51, 61, 80
Napoleon	21
Napoleonic War	20, 31
Nation building	26
NATO	17, 28, 34, 79
Navy	39
NCW	29, 49, 52, 84
Network theory	15, 57, 77, 80, 86
NGO	77, 78, 79, 83, 85
Non-trivial machine	63, 64
Ombudsman (military)	73
OOTW	23, 24, 26, 28, 29, 85, 86
Organizational theory	15, 18, 19, 57, 65, 82, 86
Peace keeping	26
Peace operations	15, 29, 43, 50, 57, 76, 79, 83, 84, 85
Peace support	26
Principal-Agent (theory)	60, 61
Problem	40
Projekttaktik	75
Prussian Army	21, 39

Quasi-heterarchy	69, 70, 73, 74, 76	System theory	15, 57, 58, 63, 71
Reciprocity	67, 78	*Tattein*	33
Related operation	24	Terrorism	23, 24, 29
RMA	77		
ROE	24, 29, 52, 83, 84	Three block war	26
		Trivial machine	63
Russian Army	21	Trust	5, 15, 31, 44, 49, 50, 51, 60, 61, 63, 64, 68, 80
Self-initiative	52, 58, 63		
Self-reference	51		
Self-regulation	15, 46, 57, 58, 63	UN	27, 79
		US Army	16, 21
Small war	20, 26	War on Terror	26
Strategic corporal	30, 73	*Zweckprogrammierung*	63, 64, 84, 85
Strategic private	30, 73		

ACKNOWLEDGEMENT

The author would like to thank Prof. Dr. Paul T. Mitchell, Brigadier-General (Ret'd) Dr. Bernd A. Goetze and Prof. Dr. Chris Madsen from the Department of Defence Studies of the Royal Military College of Canada located at the Canadian Forces College, Toronto, as well as Prof. Dr. Klaus Bellmann from the Center of Market-Oriented Product and Production Management of the Johannes Gutenberg University of Mainz, for their support in writing this paper.

Carola Hartmann Miles-Verlag

Politik, Gesellschaft, Militär

Dietrich Ungerer, *Der militärische Einsatz. Bedrohung – Führung – Ausbildung,* Potsdam 2003.

Jens Bargmann, *Ethik in der Offizierausbildung,* Münster 2004.

Silvio Gödickmeier, Martin Schlossmacher, *Soldatenfamilien im Einsatz,* Berlin 2006.

Hans-Günter Fröhling, *Innere Führung und Multinationalität,* Berlin 2006.

Christian Walther, *Im Auftrag für Freiheit und Frieden. Versuch einer Ethik für Soldaten der Bundeswehr,* Berlin 2006.

Rüdiger Schönrade, *General Joachim von Stülpnagel und die Politik,* Berlin 2007.

Uwe Hartmann, *Innere Führung. Erfolge und Defizite der Führungsphilosophie für die Bundeswehr,* Berlin 2007.

Uwe Hartmann, Claus von Rosen, Christian Walther (Hrsg.), *Jahrbuch Innere Führung 2009. Die Rückkehr des Soldatischen,* Eschede 2009.

Uwe Hartmann (ed.), *Connecting NATO. NCSA under the leadership of Lieutenant General Ulrich H. Wolf,* Berlin 2009.

Helmut R. Hammerich, Uwe Hartmann, Claus von Rosen (Hrsg.), *Jahrbuch Innere Führung 2010. Die Grenzen des Militärischen,* Berlin 2010.

Ingo Werners, *Fahren, Funken, Feuern. Hinweise für die Einsatzvorbereitung,* Berlin 2010.

Peter Heinze, *Bundeswehr „erobert" Deutschlands Osten,* Berlin 2010.

Reinhard Schneider, *Neuste Nachrichten aus unseren Kolonien. Pressemeldungen von den Aufständen in Deutsch-Ostafrika und Deutsch-Südwestafrika 1905-1906,* Berlin 2010.

Dieter E. Kilian, *Politik und Militär in Deutschland. Die Bundespräsidenten und Bundeskanzler und ihre Beziehung zu Soldatentum und Bundeswehr,* Berlin 2011.

Reiner Pommerin (ed.), *Clausewitz goes global. Carl von Clausewitz in the 21st Century,* Berlin 2011.

Hans-Christian Beck, Christian Singer (Hrsg.), *Entscheiden – Führen – Verantworten. Soldatsein im 21. Jahrhundert,* Berlin 2011.

Dieter E. Kilian, *Adenauers vergessener Retter – Major Fritz Schliebusch,* Berlin 2011.

Uwe Hartmann, Claus von Rosen, Christian Walther (Hrsg.), *Jahrbuch Innere Führung 2011. Ethik als geistige Rüstung für Soldaten,* Berlin 2011.

Jochen Wittmann, *Auftragstaktik – Just a command technique or the core pillar of mastering the military operational art?,* Berlin 2012.

Einsatzerfahrungen

Kay Kuhlen, *Um des lieben Friedens willen. Als Peacekeeper im Kosovo,* Eschede 2009.

Sascha Brinkmann, Joachim Hoppe (Hrsg.), *Generation Einsatz, Fallschirmjäger berichten ihre Erfahrungen aus Afghanistan,* Berlin 2010.

Schwitalla, Artur, *Afghanistan, jetzt weiß ich erst… Gedanken aus meiner Zeit als Kommandeur des Provincial Reconstruction Team FEYZABAD,* Berlin 2010.

Romane
Christoph Karich, *Bewährung im Grünen Meer,* Berlin 2009.
Robert B. Thiele, *Die Treuhänderin,* Berlin 2012.

Erinnerungen
Blue Braun, *Erinnerungen an die Marine 1956-1996,* Berlin 2012.
Harald Volkmar Schlieder, *Kommando zurück!,* Berlin 2012.

Monterey Studies
Uwe Hartmann, *Carl von Clausewitz and the Making of Modern Strategy,* Potsdam 2002.

Zeljko Cepanec, *Croatia and NATO. The Stony Road to Membership,* Potsdam 2002.

Ekkehard Stemmer, *Demography and European Armed Forces,* Berlin 2006.

Sven Lange, *Revolt against the West. A Comparison of the Current War on Terror with the Boxer Rebellion in 1900-01,* Berlin 2007.

Klaus M. Brust, *Culture and the Transformation of the Bundeswehr,* Berlin 2007.

Donald Abenheim, *Soldier and Politics Transformed,* Berlin 2007.

Michael Stolzke, *The Conflict Aftermath. A Chance for Democracy: Norm Diffusion in Post-Conflict Peace Building,* Berlin 2007.

Frank Reimers, *Security Culture in Times of War. How did the Balkan War affect the Security Cultures in Germany and the United States?,* Berlin 2007.

Michael G. Lux, *Innere Führung – A Superior Concept of Leadership?,* Berlin 2009.

Marc A. Walther, *HAMAS between Violence and Pragmatism,* Berlin 2010.

Frank Hagemann, *Strategy Making in the European Union,* Berlin 2010.

Ralf Hammerstein, *Deliberalization in Jordan: the Roles of Islamists and U.S.-EU Assistance in stalled Democratization,* Berlin 2011.

www.miles-verlag.jimdo.com